A Bird In Your Hand

a story of ambiguous justice

: :

Jeffrey Alan John Ph.D.
Frank L. Johnson D.V.M.

LUCIDBOOKS

A Bird in Your Hand
A Story of Ambiguous Justice

Published by Lucid Books in Houston, Texas

www.LucidBooksPublishing.com

eISBN-10: 1-63296-224-1
eISBN-13: 978-1-63296-224-9
ISBN-10: 1-63296-222-5
ISBN-13: 978-1-63296-222-5

Editor: Kate Johnsen

Interior Design: Melissa Leembruggen

Cover Design: Brandon Haskins—(1988-2010)

Special Sales: Most Lucid Books titles are available in special quantity discounts. Custom imprinting or excerpting can also be done to fit special needs. Contact Lucid Books at Info@LucidBooksPublishing.com.

A Bird in Your Hand

a story of ambiguous justice

Jeffrey Alan John Ph.D.
& Frank L. Johnson D.V.M.

Table of Contents

::

Dedication

::

This book is dedicated
to all officers of the law,
particularly those
who gave their lives
in the line of duty
protecting the citizens
of our society
from the criminals
and tyranny in the world.
May they rest in peace.
May their families be comforted.

Acknowledgments

::

During the course of the past four years, we discovered that a research project of this size could not be accomplished without a great deal of assistance. People with information or access to needed documents, motivated perhaps by kindness, or compassion, yielded time and again without hesitation to our requests, no matter how trivial or complicated. We heard the same supportive phrase repeated: "That's an interesting story!"

Trying to name everyone involved in four years of discovery risks both disrespect and insult. Nevertheless, some names come to mind immediately: Barb Cannon, in the Greene County Clerk of Courts office, launched our project by finding the original transcripts of the Tucker hearing. Gillian Hill, records and information manager/archivist; Joan Donovan, records center coordinator; and Barbara Lindsey, records assistant, the keepers of the Greene County Records Center and Archives in Xenia, seemed as fascinated as we were by the stories revealed in the dusty boxes and bound volumes, and they frequently went out of their way to find documents for us. In the same category is Deanna Ulvestad, head archivist in the Greene Room of the Greene County Library, who opened the old *Xenia Daily Gazette* files and then discovered revealing documents about the Tucker case. Catherine Wilson, executive director of the Greene County Historical Society, did not hesitate to allow access to the Society's records and information, and Joan Baxter, the society's former director, met with us to provide useful background facts.

Outside of Xenia, Carolyn Blauser of London, Ohio, found valuable newspaper records in Madison County, Ohio. The staff members of the Ohio Historical Society Archives/Library proved their expertise time and again in unearthing records and obscure documentation in a prompt, professional manner. Hiram College Archivist Jennifer Morrow dug through the files of that institution for a couple of days, trying to find traces of Ernie Evans, and volunteered useful information about wartime housing accommodations near the Ravenna Arsenal. At Wright State University, Ms. Morrow's alma mater, the head of Special Collections and Archives, Dawne Dewey, opened the newly acquired *Dayton Daily News* Archives for our use. Archivist John Armstrong mined these for a treasure trove of articles and photos.

However, all of the records, documents, and photos would have been lifeless scraps without first-person accounts from our sources. We relied on phenomenal powers of memory, despite the passing of years, of many people. Notable among these is Cincinnati attorney Irving Harris, who sat with us through many interviews, found and duplicated court records, and shepherded us through legal questions and personal histories. This book is a tribute to Mr. Harris's energy. At the opposite corner of the state, special thanks goes out to June Marie Hill, who patiently endured an extended interview and then many followup questions, and to David and Judy Hill of Garrettsville, Ohio, who generously opened their home to a stranger from Southwest Ohio, bearing odd questions about old memories. Your help, and the photo you provided, bring life to this book. Lively commentary also came from Bill and Barbara Preston of Brown County, Ohio, whose fond memories of their former neighbor Earl Tucker filled gaps and gave surprising dimensions to the narrative of a troubled life.

These tales are available to you, the reader, through the craft of writing. It has been a wonderful exercise aided immeasurably by wise, thoughtful, and all-too-gentle critics. First among these critics are Dixon Otto of Perry, Ohio, and William Hanks, Ph.D., of Covington, Kentucky, who read and re-read scrambled versions of this story that eventually became a book. Gentlemen, we would not have initiated nor continued this project without your great comments and encouragement. Thank you. And when the subsequent rough-hewn manuscript needed polish, Jack Smith of Kettering, Ohio, with Lori Davis and the Gem City Writers Group, gave us a thorough story critique and wise character insight.

We learned from this book project that publishing is serious business. The depth and size of the task meant that fundamental thanks are owed to Dean Charles Taylor of the Wright State University College of Liberal Arts, who generously approved administrative arrangements and Professional Development Leave that granted the most precious of commodities, time to do the work. At the other end of the timeline, thanks go to Melissa Leembruggen, whose encouragement and support made the creation of this book easy; Kate Johnsen, a firm and understanding editor; and the late Brandon Haskins, chief creative officer and writing instrument expert, whose design expertise enhanced this production immeasurably.

Of course, this project would have been quite a miserable task without support on the home front. Pat Johnson has been our fearless proofreader and sustenance. Karin Avila-John has patiently endured innumerable re-tellings of the story of Ernie Evans and Clarence Earl Tucker with nary a pinch nor poke. Words cannot measure our heartfelt thanks to you.

A Bird in Your Hand

a story of ambiguous justice

Jeffrey Alan John Ph.D.
& Frank L. Johnson D.V.M.

"He is like
a bird in your hand
today. You can crush his hopes
and with that you crush him,
or you can open your hand
and allow him to go free."

: :

Irving Harris
February 10, 1967

Preface

::

This story is true. It's about two young misfits from Cincinnati who, after some years of youthful petty crime, found themselves imprisoned for murder. But there's a great deal more to this true crime story than just crime and punishment. It's about a silver-haired judge and his protege; a zealous, musical prosecutor; a bold young attorney; a roller-skating queen; and a quiet midwestern community.

How do I know these things? I know about them because I was born in the community and grew up there. My father, the Honorable Judge Frank Lee Johnson, presided over this murder trial and sentenced the two young men. Dad had never been presented with a capital murder case, in which the death sentence could be rendered, and the possibility of sending two young men to the electric chair burdened his mind terribly. The incident bothered my father more than any of the other cases he ever heard.

At the time of the crime, I was serving in the U.S. Navy aboard the destroyer *USS Brush DD745* in the South Pacific. Letters from my parents show the concern that my father, the Judge, had about the fate of the two young men, and also a worry that after my discharge I might return to society with a hardened mindset and become a criminal like them. I explained in my letters that they should not worry about me. My values had not changed, although through my experiences, I had matured rather quickly.

After my discharge, I enrolled at The Ohio State University and graduated in 1952 from The College of Veterinary Medicine. I am now retired and living in Kettering, Ohio, where at a dinner party I met Jeffrey Alan John, an associate professor of journalism at Wright State University, who became my good friend, mentor, and co-author. Jeff had worked for my town's newspaper and covered the small farming communities that surrounded it. His duties included gathering news from a hamlet where, according to court testimony, the two boys introduced themselves to the county's law enforcement community. Jeff and I exchanged notes, and this book is the result.

Our story begins just after World War II. Imagine a time when you could buy a house for about $5,000, a beer in a bar for a dime, and a pack of cigarettes for fourteen cents. There were no personal computers, televisions or handheld electronics like iPods or cell phones, and telephones didn't use touch tone; some didn't even have a rotary dial. To make a phone call, you simply lifted the receiver off its hook and waited for the operator to ask, "What number, please?"

Although the United States had just won the "Good War," 1946 was a troubled time in the USA. Veterans were returning home, but jobs were hard to find. The war contracts were being cancelled, so factory workers were being laid off, and the country was plagued with labor strife.

It has been more than sixty years since the events described in this book, and the research has therefore been challenging. But Jeff and I have documented everything in the following chapters with court testimony, newspaper articles, archival materials, official documents, and personal interviews of friends and family members still living.

Nonfiction literature adheres to the premise that it conveys factual information. At the same time, however, while writing the material, the author is expected to paint pictures of events rather than simply relate the story. It is difficult to paint a portrait with a broken brush or a soiled canvas, but we have learned enough to draw some fine edges on previously ghostly images. We know the boys were looking for a weekend of good times in Northeast Ohio, but they found little fun. Disgruntled and probably disappointed, the pair started home on a Monday afternoon, and before dawn broke Tuesday morning, one of the pair shot and killed a deputy sheriff. The other boy stood and watched, but both young men were convicted of the murder and sentenced to life in the Ohio Penitentiary.

Why is all this significant? This story puts us in the shoes of "a frightened young man in hostile surroundings," to use the words of a contemporary news report. It's a narrative that over time has involved legal precedents as wide-ranging as the Miranda and Sheppard cases right at home in a small heartland community. And it's a tale that includes an inmate convicted of murder working at the Ohio State Governor's Mansion, a bit of Ohio tradition that continues to be controversial even today.

What thread ties all these narratives together? That's the essence and story of this book.

Introduction

::

My life as a criminal had a fearful ending. I was around thirteen years old at the time. Downtown, a store sold balsa-wood airplane kits and other hobby supplies, and I was mesmerized by a model of a cannon there. I had to have it. Unfortunately, it cost $1.75, a huge sum that I did not have.

So, while no one was looking, I slipped the box up under my coat and fled. All went well until I reached Donges Drug Store about two blocks away, where I encountered a cousin with her six-month-old son in a baby buggy. I relaxed my guard, holding the purloined toy in my hand as I played with the baby.

I felt a firm rap on my shoulder. "Take it back," said a stern and threatening voice. The man I turned to face worked in the store, saw the cannon, and knew I could not have paid for it. I am certain the blood drained from my frightened mug.

Then, to compound the crime, I lied. With shaking knees, I told the clerk that I had made a promise to the store's owner to come to the store the following Saturday and pay for the toy.

I believe the next seven days were some of the worst of my life to that point. In order to raise the money due, I went all over town with a red wagon, collecting bric-a-brac that I sold to the local junkyard. That Saturday, trembling and sure that everyone was watching, I put the money on the counter at the store and told the store owner that it was for the cannon I got last week. "Thank you," was all he said, as he took the money.

Frank L. "Sonny" Johnson and his father, Judge Frank Johnson, circa 1940 (Photo courtesy of Frank L. Johnson)

I have no proof, but I believe the owner had placed a call to my father, Judge Frank Johnson, to tell him that I was a thief. It would have been much like my father to suggest waiting to see what I would do. Dad would have suggested that I could just "sit in my own stew." I never asked my father if he knew about the incident, and he never mentioned it. All I know is that the situation cured me of any tendency toward crime.

: :

That wisdom was revealed to me on the streets of Xenia, the county seat of Greene County, Ohio. The name Xenia is taken from the Greek word "xenos," meaning the rights of a guest, or hospitality. The *X* is pronounced as a *Z*, so the name is heard as if it were spelled Zenia. Today, the community is recognized as a city nearly wiped out by a class-five tornado in April 1974. It killed more than thirty people, including three-year-old Theresa Cross, the granddaughter of a cousin who lived in our home.

In 1946, Xenia had a population of around 11,000. Although today it might be called a bedroom community for the larger city of Dayton, fifteen miles to the west, in the mid-1940s there was no suburban sprawl. Xenia was self-contained, so that people walked to work. Everyone was used to walking: a war had just ended; gasoline was rationed during the war, and locals were used to "hoofing it—on shank's ponies." Rent control was still in place, and friends were locked into a charge of $11 per month for their two-bedroom, second-floor apartment. There were no credit cards, no restrooms for the disabled. Retail stores closed nightly at 6:00 p.m., and on Wednesdays all the stores, professional offices, county and city offices, closed at noon. Downtown Xenia on Wednesday afternoons resembled a ghost town. No cars, no people. Nothing moved.

Saturday evenings, stores stayed open until 9:00 p.m. to allow farmers and rustic country bumpkins a chance to shop, shoot billiards, play poolroom rummy, or perhaps go bowling in the town's only bowling alley, a second-floor establishment with only three lanes. To get to it, you had to take the creaky stairs up from the street, because there were no elevators to upper floors in Xenia.

Besides the pool hall gambling, the city harbored a bookmaker and a numbers racket. It is unlikely officials were "on the take;" it is more likely that they tolerated these activities because of the lingering effects of the pre-war Great Depression and Prohibition. The county and city were conservative and Republican. People made a living without interference.

Drugs, alcohol, and crime were not issues. The entire county had a sheriff and three deputies to cover an area of about 400 square miles. Local residents who consumed alcohol partied behind closed doors or drawn shades. As far as I could tell, my father, Judge Johnson, and my mother, Ruth, would on rare occasions have a small glass of sherry.

Starting at Courthouse Square, the business district extended for two blocks in each direction. The intersection of Main Street, going east and west, and Detroit Street, going north and south was the center of town. Xenia's claim to fame in those days was its set of active railroad tracks that ran down the middle of Detroit Street through the business district. A train would pass through town twice a day, once in the morning and once at about four or five in the evening. "It would block traffic for a half an hour. It was really, really slow," recalled county commissioner Jim Ford.

Xenia High School boasted, rightfully so, of being the home of the 1942 Ohio State Basketball Champions.

The major industry was The Hooven and Allison Rope Mill, with its surrounding factory-owned homes for employees. As late as 1940, a few of the homes were still without electricity. Residents without electricity used ice boxes instead of refrigerators, and milk was delivered to the door in a milk wagon. Most furnaces were fired with coal, leaving black dust around the houses when deliveries were made. Residential neighborhoods were dotted with small, family-owned groceries and meat markets, where credit was extended to customers and grocers offered free home deliveries.

The town had two lumber yards, a junkyard, an ice company, several dairies, a foundry, and a public swimming pool—a public swimming pool open to whites only.

By 1946, African Americans comprised about a quarter of Xenia's population, and Columbus Avenue, four blocks east of the courthouse, informally divided the town between the white majority and the black residents living in the east end. This African American population, sizable for a Midwest community like Xenia, grew in proximity to the nation's first private black institution of higher education, Wilberforce College, which the Methodist Episcopal Church had founded in 1856 on property a few miles east of Xenia. With the added influence of many prominent abolitionists and Quakers about the time of the Civil War, the area became a center for the Underground Railway; around seven stops were known to have been located in the village of Wilberforce alone.

The substantial presence of the African American community had only a moderate impact on Xenia's midwestern society, however. Jim Ford, who in 1964 became Greene County's first elected African American County Commissioner, said that traditionally the county sheriff had to represent the black community among the three deputies in the county. "You had to have a black deputy to get elected," Ford said.

On the other hand, the two races got along in what was then considered a "tolerable fashion." Blacks were not served at the tables in Xenia's two most popular restaurants, Geyer's and the Candy Kitchen. Nor could they go into the first-run movie theaters, the Ohio and the Xenia; black citizens were given space only behind a rope barrier at the back of the second-run Orpheum.

In the early 1940s, local residents and students at both Wilberforce College and Antioch College in the nearby town of Yellow Springs, Ohio, began to dispute those conditions.

First, a Syrian woman named Minnie Ball, owner of a restaurant on East Main Street, sued and won $50 in damages against the owners of the Xenia Theater in 1941, when she and a friend were refused admission there.

Then, students from the local colleges began to debate the Jim Crow conditions, and on the evening of Saturday, January 30, 1943, a group of white and African American students blocked the line of patrons for the Xenia's "Bank Night," a popular weekly promotion, prompting the closure of the box office. Angry whites, armed with clubs and bottles, attacked the students on the courthouse lawn across the street; the violence was finally quelled by the arrival of local police assisted by military and state police later that night.

Authorities decided to close the Xenia for a week, and Municipal Court Judge, Dan M. Aultman, fined six people, including one African American student, $50 each for disorderly conduct. The Xenia was reopened to all its citizens the following Friday, just in time for the Xenia premier of *Casablanca*.

The initial legal action in those conflicts, Minnie Ball's lawsuit, was heard in Greene County's Common

Pleas Court, where my father, Judge Frank Lee Johnson, Sr., presided. As a judge, he was compassionate and lenient, and he was respected for his views. He was proud of the fact that none of his decisions were ever overturned by a higher court, and that he held a license to practice before the U.S. Supreme Court.

In February 1946, this white-haired judge found himself hearing his first capital murder case. The letters we exchanged showed that it worried him greatly, and besides the upcoming trial, his oldest child, Nancy, was starting to show signs of mental illness. To get away, he and Ruth fled Xenia for a little R&R in Florida. They attended the races at Hialeah Race Track in Miami, hoping a little sunshine and the races would take his mind off of his problems for a couple of weeks. Meanwhile, back home, Xenia prepared for one of the most unusual court cases in its history.

Chapter 1

::

The wail of a siren piqued Marcus Walker's curiosity as he ate his breakfast alone in Minnie Ball's little restaurant. Walker stopped there almost every morning, before he caught the bus to work in Dayton. It was a nice place to grab a warm cup of coffee, and Minnie welcomed black men as customers. The same couldn't be said of many other eating places in town.

When he heard the siren, Walker got up, went to the window, and watched as a late-model Buick sedan and the sheriff's '41 Pontiac stopped at the intersection in front of the restaurant.

"I seen one car pull up, and the other car was behind," he testified later in court.

"Someone got out of the police car, but who it was I didn't know. So I didn't pay no more attention."

Walker continued on in testimony, "About a second later I heard a shot, and a short time after that I heard several shots."

Upstairs, in the bedroom of an apartment above the restaurant, George Sams also was alerted by the loud police siren blaring in the early morning. He quickly raised the Venetian blinds of his window, and in the dim pool of illumination there under the streetlights, he saw a car marked "Greene County Sheriff," and heard "a little talking, then all of a sudden some gunfire."

As he watched, a man staggered backward, stumbled when his feet hit the curb, and fell against a sign post.

About 300 feet away, on the other side of Main Street, Lawrence Byrd lay awake in his bed, listening to the *Reveille Roundup* show on the radio. At about 5:00 a.m., he heard a siren and thought to himself that the State Highway Patrol had made another stop on Route 42, probably close to the corner. Then he heard a gunshot, followed by a pause and several more shots. He sprang up, ran out of his room, and collided with his sister, who also had heard the noise.

"Somebody's shot," she said.

A block away, south of the intersection, Isaiah Rose heard what he thought to be a truck's backfire as he walked north on Columbus Street. He was on schedule to take the Dayton-Xenia bus to work, but about midway up the block an extraordinary scene surprised him. Joe Anderson, an acquaintance who was the night jailer and the County Sheriff Department's only black deputy, limped out of a gas station at the intersection, preceded by a young white man with his hands in the air.

Rose was glad to know Anderson. Rose thought it exceptional and fortunate that Xenia even had a black man like himself on the police force, and besides, Joe Anderson was genial and understanding. He was a real professional, even if he hadn't yet been issued a real uniform. But this morning, he wore a pained grimace.

It was a strange scene Rose encountered when he walked into the intersection: the hobbling Anderson and the boy with his arms in the air, and two men lying in the street. One, a uniformed police officer half on the sidewalk, groaned a few times and then was motionless. The other lay in the street, writhing and asking for help. Anderson pushed the young man he was guiding toward Rose.

"I'm hit. I'm bleeding," Anderson said. "I don't know how bad I'm hurt—how far from passing out. I'm going to go get help."

"I'll go, Joe," Rose offered, but Anderson shook him off. "I can ride faster than you can walk," the wounded man said. Then he startled Rose by handing him a small revolver.

"Is it any good?" Rose asked, peering at the weapon. Anderson broke down the gun and in the growing light of dawn the two men saw that all five rounds had been fired. Anderson then produced a larger police gun from his coat pocket. "If he moves, kill him," Anderson said as he handed it to Rose, whose first thought was how white folks would respond if they saw him aiming a gun at this white youngster.

Then the deputy climbed into the parked sheriff's cruiser and sped off, leaving the baffled Rose, his captive, and the two wounded victims lying on the street. Some bystanders sifted onto the scene, eyeing Rose suspiciously, and the boy on the ground squirmed.

"C'mere and take a look. Where'm I hit?" the young man pleaded. "Where'm I hit?"

Minutes later—it seemed like hours to Rose—Anderson's cruiser returned, followed closely by a Xenia

Police cruiser. Anderson had gone the few blocks west on Main Street to the courthouse, turned right, and almost immediately encountered Patrolman John King, who had answered a telephone call from a woman about a shooting at Columbus and Main. King recognized Anderson in the Greene County car, and the deputy motioned for the officer to follow in a Xenia car. The two cars halted about a hundred feet away from the intersection of Columbus Avenue and Main Street, where Anderson struggled from the car and announced, "Confer's shot, and I'm shot, too."

King saw a black man standing at the intersection, holding a gun in a threat against a young white fellow with his hands in the air. A boy on the ground said, "Loosen my belt, would you?" but King ignored the request and stepped past him to the still body in a slouched sitting position against a sign post. It was Earl Confer, a sheriff's deputy well-known in the community. The officer found no pulse.

"He did a good job," King said. "Earl's gone."

Within minutes, Sergeant Ancil Stephens of the Xenia Police Department arrived. He saw King and Rose holding guns on a ruffled young man who stood with arms in the air, another youth in the middle of the street, and Deputy Confer lying against the curb. Stephens detected no sign of life in Confer. There was nothing he could do but cover the body with a blanket. The only ambulance in town, operated by the Neeld Funeral Home, was summoned and arrived in a few minutes. A stretcher bearing the wounded boy was inserted, followed by Anderson, and the two were taken to Xenia's private McClellan Hospital.

There was discussion about moving Confer's body, but the officers agreed that the county coroner should examine the scene first.

Stephens ordered Officer King to direct morning traffic that was beginning to accumulate, and two waiting trucks were ushered through the intersection. Then Sgt. Stephens handcuffed the young man Isaiah Rose had been guarding and shoved him into a Xenia cruiser for a ride to the police station. After handing the prisoner over to the jailers, Stephens returned to the green Buick still parked against the curb. In a cursory study of the car, he made an interesting discovery: an old shotgun, loaded, lay on the floor of the back seat. It would become a pivotal element in a gathering prosecution.

Chapter 2

::

More than a half century has passed since my father's death, but just a few years ago, his words startled me. I had dumped out the contents of the archives envelope for Case Number 8101, and there on the desk, folded among the yellowing old documents, lay a pointedly abrupt letter he had written in 1953 to a Cincinnati attorney.

I wondered if the attorney was still alive, so after dinner, I checked the phone book, found the name, and called. To the woman who answered, I explained that I was looking for information about a court case following a murder in 1946. "My, that was a long time ago," she said. Then her husband came into the conversation, and we made arrangements to meet.

We chose as our rendezvous a corner restaurant in a pleasant upscale Cincinnati neighborhood. Trees shaded the sidewalk café tables that noon hour under a beautiful blue sky. Shoppers and well-dressed business people strolled by; empty tables far outnumbered the lunchtime diners. Traffic noise prompted my co-author and me to move indoors to wait.

Jeff and I confronted darkness when we entered. The room had flat black walls, and my eyes had to adjust to the stark contrast with the bright outdoors; only a streak or two of midday light streamed in through drawn Venetian blinds. The place was nearly empty but for a lone woman at a small table in the back, by a window.

We sat near the front door where we could be seen. A waiter served us water, and we reviewed our notes about the crime and the subsequent legal battles that had brought us here.

Our thoughts were interrupted by the sight of a compact, dapper older fellow carrying a ponderous bound volume. Wearing a gray suit, a striped red tie, and a white starched shirt with cuff links, Irving Harris looked the part of a successful lawyer, and we rose to intercept him. After proper introductions, we found he was happy to talk about this old case.

Harris's voice was crisp and inviting, his memory phenomenal, and his dark eyes sparkled as he recalled the case of Clarence Earl Tucker. Reliving the memories enlivened and delighted the veteran attorney. "He was a nice kid," Harris said. "But for the first week or so in jail he was treated really badly."

Harris sat back, and his face turned grim. "Those two Cincinnati cops were really bad news. They could have been killers themselves. I remember one of them was tough. And the other, the German one, was always nicely dressed, with slicked-back hair. He was so smooth."

: :

All the records we've found say that Adolph Mezger, the "German one," was a good cop, as standards went in 1946. He had joined the force in 1911 and, as a police officer, his job was important enough he didn't have to march off to war in 1917 like so many of his buddies. He was 66 years old at the time of the Xenia incident; several years earlier, he could have retired with longevity, but he had been assigned to the criminal investigation division as a detective, a step up and off the street.

Mezger was as handsome and suave as a matinee idol. He wore silk suits and stylish broad-rimmed hats that covered his coal-black, oiled hair combed back over his ears in ducktail fashion. Mezger lived next to the Over-the-Rhine district on Spring Street in the downtown area of Cincinnati, and he belonged. He knew almost everyone in the area, the good and the bad, and with his deep knowledge of the community, he could be a valuable friend or a vicious foe. The questions he asked of his suspects were always made with soft-spoken words, yet they carried an unspoken threat of force.

His longtime partner, Millard Schath, was twenty years his junior. Schath had joined the Cincinnati Police Department in 1924, after service in the U.S. Navy. In 1920, as a gunner's mate on the submarine *USS S-5,* he was among its crew of thirty-five men who were trapped at the bottom of the Atlantic for more than twenty-four hours when the sub couldn't surface. "Scared? No," he told reporters years later. "It was only a stuck valve."

"He knows no fear," a colleague on the police force once said. "With Schath on your side you felt safe." For good reason: Schath was known to be quick to use his gun, and by the time he retired in 1951, he had killed four men and had taken part in the shooting deaths of two others. "Never give a crook a break, or they'll get you first," he proclaimed as his motto. Schath was like a bulldog: strong, unrelenting by nature and, at times, fierce. With a solid six-foot frame, dark eyes, and menacing smile, he was quite an intimidator.

The pair, Mezger and Schath, worked together in almost choral harmony. Here was a raging bull, pacing back and forth on one side of an interrogated suspect. On the other side sat the quiet tormentor, slowly taking in a drag from a cigarette. Mezger would sit calmly on the edge of a desk and offer the person he was interrogating a smoke. He would appear to be at ease, relaxed. Schath was abrupt, direct, to the point, and impatient with the answers given.

According to local rumors—whispers the pair encouraged—Schath and Mezger could back up their threats with serious action. Their beats included several Cincinnati hotels, and once two hoods who were members of Detroit's notorious and bloodthirsty Purple Gang signed into the Metropole Hotel, an establishment covered by the two detectives. According to the tale, the punks tried to muscle their way into Cincinnati's underworld, and Mezger and Schath paid a visit. One of the guests ended up being hanged by his heels out of his hotel window. The message was clear: you're not welcome, and don't ever come back.

The morning of January 29, 1946, Mezger and Schath were en route to Dayton, a couple hours north of Cincinnati. Detective Chief Clem Merz had sent them to get information about the assault and robbery of gas station attendant Fred Mitchell, who had agreed to accompany the detectives and try to identify three men held by Dayton police.

For the detectives, the trip made this morning special. They would get a chance to eat a nice lunch, perhaps at Dayton's popular King Cole or the Mandarin Room, and charge it to the department. With any luck, the identification and interrogation could be over by noon. Then, they could relax, have a couple of drinks, eat lunch, and mosey back home before rush hour.

As they were nearing Dayton, the squawk box on the dash blared a demand that the detectives call headquarters. Mezger pulled the car into a service station, made the call, and returned to the car.

"We have to go to Xenia," he said. "Two punks from Cincinnati killed a deputy this morning. The Sheriff there thinks we might know 'em."

Their passenger, Fred Mitchell, interrupted them by saying the news was an amazing coincidence. "This truck driver at my place this morning told me these two tough guys left the restaurant about five, and by the time he got to Xenia, the cops was directing traffic around a car that was blockin' the street."

"He claimed he saw a body layin' in the crosswalk, but I thought it was bullshit."

It was mid-morning when the threesome arrived in Xenia and went directly to the century-old county jail building in the center of town. While Mitchell cooled his heels in an outer office, Mezger and Schath introduced themselves to Sheriff Walton Spahr and told him they had come to question his new prisoner about some crimes in Cincinnati. They would gladly question the suspect about the shooting if the Sheriff thought it would help. The two detectives followed Spahr into his office, where they heard details about the murder of the deputy early that morning.

After a few minutes a disheveled, sleepy-lidded youth limped into the room, and he immediately recognized the detectives. Clarence Earl Tucker was more frightened than he had ever been in his life. In the rising light of dawn that morning, as a cop tossed him roughly onto the back seat of a police cruiser, Tucker had seen someone pull a blanket over the head of the officer who fell when his buddy Ernie shot him. Tucker also knew that both Ernie, as well as the black deputy who had held him briefly at gunpoint, had been shot. That meant Tucker was the only available witness to the tragedy.

Chapter 3

::

Her given name was June Marie Edwards, but her family, friends, and classmates called her "Junie." The 1945 yearbook for Freedom (Ohio) High School described her as "mischievous and vivacious, a cheerleader with a cute smile. Interest: boys." The yearbook didn't mention that roller-skating was Junie's passion. Her older brother, Harris, who managed the community skating rink, wanted her to skate professionally.

One wartime Saturday night, Junie put on her pleated skirt, penny loafers, and a light jacket and walked the half-mile to the rink, her white-tasseled skates slung over her shoulder. It was time to go skating. She paid her twenty-five cents admission—money from babysitting—and entered the skating floor, a world where the slender Junie became graceful.

All the young men in the area waited to skate with her. This night, as Junie started to practice her turns, she noticed a good-looking young man in uniform. He was laughing, joking, and flirting with all the girls who would skate with him, but he wasn't a good skater. Nevertheless, Junie soon found herself flirting and trying to teach him to skate. He laughed a lot and didn't seem to take life seriously, "a happy-go-lucky kind of guy," Junie remembered, years later. When they took a break and found a bench to share, he introduced himself as Ernie Evans. He told her he was an Air Corps cadet in pre-flight training at Hiram College, and he had hitched a ride to the rink for some fun.

She asked him where he was from. "Cincinnati," he replied.

: :

The city that Ernie Evans called home has a long history of what we now call *diversity*. In the eighteenth century the area's unbroken wooded wilderness attracted settlers and then trading and business interests that formed a commercial center.

But as cities age, they evolve. Eventually, the quaint working-class neighborhoods age and degenerate over time. Cincinnati's were no exception. Built along the Ohio River, the older communities that became the center city are settled amid hills, so that they freeze in the chill winters and steam in the humid summers. As the metropolis grew, those who could afford it moved to the hilltops to escape the stench from the stockyards, the odors of industry, and the pall and coal soot from both smoky chimneys and straining locomotives. The wealthy enjoyed the cool nighttime breezes afforded by the hilltops, while the laboring classes endured the stagnant air of tenement life in the city.

The Over-the-Rhine district in Cincinnati is one of those old, ethnic neighborhoods. The community, originally settled by German immigrants with a little mix of other ethnic groups, varies in architectural styles from just plain American, with its sturdy brick buildings built side-by-side, to some Bavarian and Italian Renaissance styles.

By the late nineteenth century, beer gardens and gaiety animated the community; in the center of the neighborhood stood the Findlay Street Market, where a grand parade originates even now for every Opening Day, the renewal of each major league baseball season. A festive day for all of Cincinnati, the celebration winds through the streets of the city to the home field of the Cincinnati Reds. In the early years, the celebration ended at nearby Redland Park, soon renamed Crosley Field.

In those days, the Reds, uplifted by the superb pitching of Johnny VanderMeer, won the National League pennant and played in the 1940 World Series against the Detroit Tigers. My father, the Judge, took me to a World Series game that fall, and we bought a miniature baseball bat with a Reds pennant attached. Meanwhile, teenaged buddies Ernie Evans and Clarence Earl Tucker, who had grown up in the neighborhood, stalked old ladies on the area's streets for purses they could easily snatch.

Both Evans and Tucker were born in the summer of 1925, roughly 2,000 miles apart. Tucker was born in Oregon on August 15 of that year, the son of Earl Claude Tucker and the grandson of a former railroad telegraph operator who had moved from Minnesota to Douglas County, Oregon, before 1920. There, the grandfather, his wife, and two young sons farmed rented land.

When Earl Claude Tucker was twenty-two, he married a sixteen-year-old Canadian, Eileen Schumacher. A year later, they had a son. The young couple named him Clarence, and for a middle name, they took his father's name, Earl.

The family lived in Maxville, a lumber camp in Wallowa County, Oregon, where the elder Earl Tucker worked in the timber industry as a "top decker," a climber who sawed off the top section of a tree before it was felled. The dangerous work, all by hand saws, required dexterity and great upper body strength. He developed huge forearms and acquired the nickname "Popeye."

By the time of the 1930 census, Eileen Tucker had moved to Portland, Oregon, to live in a Salvation Army Home. Documents suggest she may have been pregnant, and that by then, she may have been separated from her husband, and destitute.

For young Clarence Earl Tucker, between his birth and 1932, three separate events occurred that altered his fate. First, Eileen left the family, and news arrived that she had died. Then the young Tucker developed poliomyelitis, which weakened his left leg and ankle giving him a decided limp for the rest of his life. Lastly, the stock market crashed in October 1929, propelling the United States into the Great Depression of the '30s and forcing Popeye Tucker, with his young son, out of the forests of the Northwest.

Fifty years later, Cincinnati attorney Irving Harris, hired by Popeye to defend his son, called the elder Tucker "an unlikely father." Yet, in order to get help to raise his motherless child, Popeye moved cross-country to the city of Cincinnati and into the crowded apartment shared by his parents, Claude and Ella, and his brother, Neal.

Thus, for the first part of his life, Clarence Earl Tucker explored and played in the vast expanse of Oregon's scenic grandeur, with rushing salmon-filled streams, towering pines, and clean air. Then he was moved to the inner city, to be raised by assorted relatives among alleys and tall tenements, obnoxious odors, and street-tough kids. His father, Popeye, remarried and eventually was able to get employment as a maintenance man in a small apartment building of brown brick with woodwork of faint Victorian influence at 1333 Bishop Street, overlooking the Cincinnati Zoo. Part of his salary was rent for a walkout basement apartment in the building, where the whole Tucker family lived within earshot of the strange noises of exotic animals.

The young Tucker boy, who by now favored his middle name, Earl, got into trouble with the law by the time he was ten years old—his crime the destruction of a stairway banister. Later, he was charged in a separate incident with malicious destruction of property. Apparently bitter and ill-tempered, he seemed to show little remorse over his actions. Possibly, Tucker resented the move away from friends in Oregon, or maybe he objected to his father's second marriage. Children in his new school may have teased the limping new kid, or shunned him.

Perhaps compensating for social ills, he learned to be adept with his hands. For the rest of his life, Clarence Earl Tucker enjoyed working with wood and building intricate model airplanes.

Eventually convicted of the malicious destruction charge, the young Earl Tucker was delivered for a time to Cincinnati's Glenview School for Boys, "a training school for socially maladjusted or 'problem' boys." He also

Clarence Earl Tucker as a young man (Photo courtesy of Wright State University, *Dayton Daily News* Archives)

attended Rothenberg Junior High and Woodward High School in Cincinnati, but by the age of fifteen, he had been arrested again, for auto theft, although the Hamilton County grand jury declined to indict him. Then he was convicted of burglary and on January 14, 1943, he was "enrolled" at the Ohio Boys Industrial School, the reformatory in Lancaster, Ohio. Nine months later, on October 21, Tucker was paroled and released to his grandfather, Claude. By now a strapping five feet, ten inches tall and weighing just over 150 pounds, the blonde, blue-eyed teenager was surely hardened and street-wise. He did not return to school; it had gained him nothing, except his only close friend, Ernie Evans.

: :

Ernest Finley Evans was born in Kentucky on July 7, 1925. At the time of his birth, Ernie's family included parents Joseph Grant Evans and his wife, Alice. Additionally, there were three brothers named Ernest, Grant Jr., and James, and finally an older sister, Edna Mae. They all lived together in the small rural village of Visalia in Kenton County in 1930.

It's difficult to find the little hollow of Visalia, which is located on the west bank of the Licking river fifteen miles south of Covington, Kentucky. The area is hilly and wooded. Trees have reclaimed once-cultivated fields. At one time, the community boasted a population of 300, but today perhaps 150 residents remain. Boards cover the windows of the few remaining buildings. An active railroad line that once employed Ernest's father as a signalman and watchman borders the west edge of the settlement.

"There's not much left," said an elderly gentleman as he walked his dog in the area. "At one time, there was a ferry across the Licking. There were three coal yards, three groceries, and two churches. We even had our own tobacco warehouse and a twelve-acre picnic park."

By 1935, the Evans family had moved to Cincinnati and added three more daughters to the family: Betty, Anita, and Sue. In a fashion similar to the experience of the Tuckers, the Evans family moved from an unhurried lifestyle along a lazy river, where a boy could wander and fish in a rural setting of rolling hills and timbered lands, to the noise, odors, and crowding of the inner city. Evans's mother, Alice, found work as a waitress on Republic Street in the Over-the-Rhine district, and the extra income helped her afford to shop for the family at the Findlay Street Market, where she could buy round steak for forty cents a pound, or a pound of ground coffee for fifty cents.

The harsh working-class neighborhoods of Cincinnati molded Ernie Evans into a handsome, intelligent young man with a brash, impetuous nature. He was soon arrested for purse snatching, larceny, burglary, and auto theft; after several warnings, he was sent to the Glenview School For Boys at about the same time as Clarence Earl Tucker. No doubt Tucker and Evans knew each other by this time. In the years just before the U.S. entered World War II, both attended Over-the-Rhine's Rothenberg Junior High School, where the principal believed in corporal punishment, and completed the ninth grade at Woodward High School.

Ernest Finley Evans, in an undated mug shot.

Then in 1942, Evans was captured during a joyriding spree in nearby Indiana, convicted, and confined just west of Indianapolis at the Plainfield Juvenile Correction Facility, a mid- to severe-level institute with a reputation for harsh discipline. (About fifteen years later, Plainfield would house, and repeatedly punish, another teenager with behavior problems, Charles Manson.) Evans soon escaped from this institution but was recaptured and returned, no doubt earning the requisite five lashes with a leather strap. In late September 1943, he enlisted in Danville, Indiana, a few miles from Plainfield, as a cadet in the Army Air Corps. Probably, everyone involved hoped the military service would straighten him out.

Deciding to join the Army Air Corps would have been typical of the daring Evans, who was impudent enough to snatch purses from women on crowded city streets. In the Air Corps, he was shipped for training to Texas as an aviation cadet private in the 59th Training Group, and then he received orders that would prove to be pivotal in his life.

Ernie Evans in his Air Corps cadet uniform

The Air Corps sent Evans and 250 Air Corps trainees to Hiram College, a tiny liberal arts school in the rolling countryside about twenty miles northeast of Akron, Ohio, and a few miles north of the huge Ravenna Arsenal, which produced TNT and other munitions for the U.S. war effort. The attraction for the Air Corps was Hiram's innovative Intensive Study Plan, under which students took one course at a time for a seven-week session, and some cadets took classes with the college's traditional students and lived in dormitories on campus. Others, according to local historian Jennifer Morrow, lived in the Maple Grove Housing Unit in the nearby community of Windham, and worked at the Arsenal.

"In those days, we didn't have many men on campus," Morrow explained, and life must have been socially comfortable for male Air Corps cadets. One in this situation was Private Evans, who one evening visited the roller-skating rink in nearby Drakesburg. It was a popular spot for young people, one of whom was the pretty auburn-haired eighteen-year-old, June Marie Edwards. She attracted the cadet's attention with her extraordinary prowess on wheels.

"I used to roller-skate a lot," she recalled many years later. "He saw me there, and we dated some. It was one of those wartime things."

June Marie Edwards, in a postwar pose (Photo courtesy of Dave & Judy Hill)

Their relationship was hardly unique. "All the girls had a sailor-boy or soldier," June remembered. Besides, both Ernie and Junie were hot commodities. "He chased around with all the girls," Junie said, and boys would stand in line to skate with her. Nevertheless, this charming, intelligent boy who looked so good in his uniform found a special place with her. "He was brilliant," she said, and apparently possessed of a golden tongue. "He called me everything sweet," June recalled. He claimed to be a pilot in training taking courses at Hiram, although records don't indicate the ninth-grade dropout was ever actually enrolled there.

They began to meet frequently at the Drakesburg skating rink, and when Junie took him home to meet her parents, her mother was enthralled—"She thought he was beautiful," June said—but her father was suspicious.

Ernie had his faults. Junie thought he was overly attached to his mother, and a bit spoiled. "He would use our phone and call home to his mother, and he seemed to think nothing of reversing the charges," she recalled, noting the contrast with her more frugal use of expensive long distance phone service.

More disturbing was his racial bigotry. Whereas she had been raised to treat all human beings as equals, Ernie seemed to have an ingrained sense of racial superiority and hatred for people of color. When they went out to dinner, he reacted with disdain if blacks were present. "He would say 'those dirty this, or dirty that,' or 'How dare that boy act like that.' He irritated me because he was so prejudiced," June said.

She overlooked these flaws to the extent that the couple began to make long-term plans. They talked about getting engaged, and he promised to look for a ring when he next went home to Cincinnati. Then, suddenly, he was transferred back to Perrin Field in Sherman, Texas, a basic training center where one of the new flight instructors was Captain Chuck Yeager, a young, hot-shot pilot just returned from the war in Europe. In 1947 as an experimental test pilot, Yeager would become the first human to break the sound barrier.

Ernie and Junie exchanged letters for a while, but he stopped writing. June recalled that after a few months, she received a strange note from a woman claiming to be Ernie's nurse at a hospital in San Antonio, Texas. He had injured his face in a plane crash, the nurse said, and he wasn't able to write. Then the war ended, and Junie received a few more letters from Ernie that she didn't have time to answer because she was enrolled in a beauty college and getting serious about preparing for her state licensing board examinations. She moved in with her friend Dee in Akron, close to the school and thought the cadet had dropped out of her life.

She couldn't have known that Ernie Evans, now discharged from the Army, was making new plans for the couple, and planning a trip north for a surprise visit.

Chapter 4

::

The Cincinnati Enquirer didn't have good news for Ernie Evans the morning of Wednesday, January 23, 1946. Woozy after a whiskey-saturated night across the Ohio River in Newport, Kentucky, he sat in the Over-the-Rhine coffee shop where his mom worked, and tried to focus on front-page stories that painted a grim picture of disarray in the city.

It seemed like every factory worker in town was on strike. Wage-earners were reacting as they watched the thaw in prices that had been frozen during the war. Everything cost more: milk was up to seventy cents a gallon, and a loaf of bread now cost a dime. About the only thing less expensive was gasoline, but people weren't driving much because hardly any new model cars were out yet to replace the worn-out heaps that had lasted through the war. In the Cincinnati area, walkouts at meatpacking plants put meat in short supply, and for about a week, a bakers' strike had kept bread and baked goods off grocery shelves—a "famine," the paper called it. Wage disputes closed General Electric, Westinghouse, and General Motors factories in the city, and steelworkers were walking off their jobs at two dozen local mills, as well as plants nationally. Things were so bad across the country, with millions of workers on strike, that President Harry Truman had put off his message to Congress for a week, until Tuesday night.

Evans had expected to find work and easy money when he was discharged from the Army Air Force two months earlier, after undistinguished service and a failed effort to earn his pilot's wings. Staring at the paper this cold January morning, he could see few legitimate jobs, but he had some other kinds of options. His disabled buddy Earl Tucker, who had a recent criminal record and even fewer prospects, had opened the door, literally, to a minor windfall for the pair.

Tucker had worked tending the furnace at the Kemper Lane Hotel, a job that allowed him to have keys to various locked rooms in the building. Using the hotel's own key-making machine, he had fashioned a duplicate key to a storeroom where liquor was kept, and on Saturday night, January 19, he told Evans about the storeroom and his key.

The following night, in the English Woods neighborhood where Evans lived, the pair stole a Buick on Westwood Northern Boulevard, switched license plates, and drove to the hotel. There Evans parked the Buick in the alley behind the hotel and listened to the Les Brown Dance Orchestra on the car radio while Tucker used his key to open a door so he could creep into the storage area. Tucker was dragging cases of liquor from the storeroom when he discovered that he was locked in; he didn't have a key to the hotel's rear entrance. He had to break the lock on the door, but eventually he struggled out under the heavy weight of fifteen cases of whiskey, which the pair successfully loaded into the stolen car.

For the next few days, they were salesmen in Newport. The two illicit liquor vendors sold some of their goods on the street and kept some for their own private use, but Tucker later recalled that most of it went to a Newport dealer. In total, they made $600, which they split 50-50.

Newport not only afforded the two boys a place to unload their whiskey, but it also offered them a haven where they could get drunk, gamble, and spend their ill-gotten loot. The town atmosphere easily absorbed their misbehavior, because in the mid '40s the city was corrupt, with gambling parlors, bookie joints, prostitution, and booze. There were everyday bookie parlors, where housewives could lose their grocery money making fifty-cent bets or parlays on the ponies, and there were high-class gambling establishments, or "supper clubs." These included the Lookout House and Beverly Hills, sophisticated establishments offering fine dining, floor shows, dancing, and plush casinos. One of the frequent patrons at Beverly Hills was my father, Judge Frank Johnson.

On Wednesdays at noon, the Greene County Courthouse closed, and the Judge would take off for Newport, sometimes with my mother and me. At first, we frequented a barber shop in the Cincinnati suburb of Fairfax. We'd walk in, say hello to Ed the proprietor, and go to a back room with a refined bookmaking establishment. My father could assess the abilities of racehorses extremely well, and both my mother and I often chose successfully as well. Afterward, we would have dinner at the Golden Lamb Inn in Lebanon, an elegant remnant of the old stagecoach route between Cincinnati and Dayton. For my father, these fine dinners were the high point of the trip.

Then Ed's place closed, and the family outings moved to the Flamingo Club in Newport. I remember it as a big place with lots of roulette, blackjack, and craps tables. My father, the Judge, became so familiar there that he had a special number that he could use to phone in wagers. He'd read *The Cincinnati Enquirer* at home in Xenia, then call the Flamingo Club and place bets using his code number. The next time we visited the club, he would collect if he won, or pay his bill if he lost.

Police raided these clubs on various occasions, but they never found any gambling equipment. The establishments were forewarned, and gambling paraphernalia just evaporated from the premises. In January 1946, for example, *The Enquirer* reported that police detectives had been dispatched to the Yorkshire Club after a client of attorney Thomas Hardesty "charged that gambling existed in the place." The Newport City Manager said that those detectives could find no gambling activity.

"The report of the so-called detectives of the Newport Police Department in regard to gambling in the Yorkshire, which they say they could not find, in my opinion is an open invitation to any and all law violators to make the city of Newport their rendezvous," Hardesty complained in his response to the city.

Ernie Evans, having taken advantage of that unstated invitation, held the remnant of what had been a wad of cash as he studied Cincinnati's bad news in mid-January

1946. It was time for a road trip, he decided. He would use the stolen Buick he and Tucker had stashed, and he would go north to Ravenna, Ohio, to rekindle his old romance with Junie Edwards. His sister Edna Mae, a member of the Women's Army Corps, was stationed near there, living with her husband and baby girl, and he and Tucker could stay at her place.

When his mother swished past him in the coffee shop with a plate full of sausage and eggs, he rose unsteadily from his stool. "Mother," he announced, "I'm going with Tucker to visit a sick friend across the river, in Manchester. I'll be gone a few days."

Alice interrupted her business with a customer. Her son had seemed so much bigger and more mature when he came home from the army, but today he looked scruffy. And she didn't think much of his idea.

"Do you have to?" she earnestly pleaded. "That boy's always up to no good. And what are you gonna use to get there?"

"Earl has a car. We'll be okay," Evans concluded. Then he went to a phone booth down the street, where his mother couldn't hear him, and called Tucker.

"Earl, I got an idea," Evans said. "Let's take that Buick and really go someplace. Let's have some fun."

"Uh, whatcha' got in mind?" Tucker responded.

'I'm thinkin' we could go up north," Evans answered. "Remember that girl I told ya about in Akron? My sister lives close up there. We could drive up there, have a good time."

"Ernie, that car's hot," Tucker whispered into the phone. "If we got caught, it'd be our asses. And what am I gonna do while you're with that babe?"

"Hey, maybe June can fix you up with a broad. C'mon, Earl. Nobody up there's gonna know the car's hot."

Tucker finally agreed. Years later, he recalled the pair discussing the kinds of mischievous adventures they might have, and what they might do if they were chased. That was when he decided to take his grandfather's old short-barreled shotgun along "just in case." The old gun Claude Tucker had sawed off years ago might come in handy; like in the movies, the one who wasn't driving could discourage pursuit by hanging out of the passenger-side window, shooting to "pepper the windshield" of a trailing car.

The pair retrieved the stolen Buick on Thursday morning. They drove straight up U.S. Route 42 to Ravenna, a village about twenty miles east of Akron. The drive took all day. When they got there, they contacted Edna Mae. By coincidence, she was working at the Ravenna Arsenal, Ernie's old stomping grounds.

On Friday afternoon, Evans persuaded Edna Mae to let him borrow her new Plymouth, while Clarence kept the Buick. Evans correctly assumed the shiny new car would impress Junie, even though Edna Mae insisted that she accompany her brother and bring along her two-year-old daughter, Constance. But when the trio arrived at Junie's home in the village of Freedom, about a half-mile from the skating rink where they had met, Evans was disappointed to learn from Junie's mother that Junie had moved closer to her school in Akron, Ohio about twenty miles away.

Junie recalls that for her mother, the prospect of taking Evans to her daughter wasn't a problem, because her mother favored the handsome ex-cadet. She offered to go with Evans, his sister, and niece to find Junie.

That evening, the sun was touching the horizon as Junie and her roommate Dee got off a bus after class. In the fading orange glow of dusk, she recognized walking toward her the boy who had left her months before, when he promised to buy an engagement ring.

She still remembers the spontaneous embrace the two shared there on the street. His surprising return was typical: "That's the way the boys were coming home," June recalls. "It was constant. Who's coming home now? You didn't know."

After the warm greeting, Junie went to the apartment she shared with Dee, gathered some clothes for the weekend, and joined the group in Edna Mae's car for the trip back to Freedom. Unfortunately, that ride home was to be the best time of the weekend for Ernie and June.

Away from the playful world of the skating rink, Junie asserted that she had to complete her cosmetology schooling. She had to repay her father for the tuition, she explained. Her independence must have crushed Ernie's plans for the pair, leaving him disillusioned. June doesn't recall meeting him again after that Friday evening.

Nevertheless, Junie's younger brother Lawrence took to the older boys, and the next morning Evans and

Tucker picked him up when they went to Minard's Sporting Goods store in Ravenna so that Tucker could buy a model airplane kit. Tucker paid for a pack of cigarettes, noticed a display of pistols, and asked clerk Wayne Porter to show him two of them. Porter produced the weapons, and Tucker later said he recognized one as a bargain. With a slightly damaged ejection mechanism, the Harrington and Richardson .38 caliber "Defender" model was available for $37. The deal included 119 cartridges and a leather holster, and Tucker said later he thought he might repair the gun and sell it back home in Cincinnati for a profit. But he didn't have enough cash to complete the deal, so he borrowed $7 from Evans and signed the registration papers as "Sam Scott" of Newport, Kentucky.

The group returned Junie's brother to Freedom, but Junie wasn't there. It was clear that Ernie had experienced trouble rekindling the old flame with Junie, and Tucker wasn't having much fun that weekend either. The Buick originally stolen in Cincinnati began to fail, and Tucker was without transportation. The pair needed another car, so Sunday evening, Tucker and Evans drove to downtown Cleveland, drank more than a few beers, and saw a Buick coupe owned by Mary Nick sitting with its engine running in front of a garage on Euclid Avenue. Opportunity knocked. Tucker hopped into the coupe and followed Evans in it, but he found that the clutch in the car was slipping badly. About the time they reached Portage County, about thirty miles southeast of Cleveland, Tucker pulled alongside Evans and told him the car wasn't worth the trouble. They parked the coupe on the road, shot holes in the gas tank, and set the car on fire. They didn't want police to find any fingerprints, Tucker recalled later.

By Monday, the pair must have decided they had had enough of Northeast Ohio. They toured Cleveland one last time, stopping for beers and lunch, and as they left, they noticed a two-tone green, four-door 1941 Buick, the most recent model available at the time, sitting in front of a Cleveland drugstore with the engine running. It was a deal these two boys simply could not pass up. This time, Evans jumped out, slipped behind the wheel of the newer car, and sped off with Tucker following. Later down the road, somewhere near Akron, Evans made a sudden stop, and Tucker smashed into the back of the newly acquired Buick, crunching the front end of the Cincinnati car. Tucker, in the damaged vehicle, lurched to a hidden area alongside a nearby railroad track, and Evans shot a hole in its gas tank, poured gasoline on the upholstery, lit a match, and cremated the remains.

They headed back to Cincinnati on U.S. Route 42. Around midnight, they encountered a distressed motorist whose car had broken down. They gave the man a lift to an all-night service station at the junction of U.S. 42 and U.S. 40 outside London, Ohio. The man later reported he noticed the sawed-off shotgun on the floor of the back seat, but said nothing; these guys offered a much-needed lift, and besides, it was none of his business. After their passenger got a repair part, Tucker and Evans drove him back to his car, then proceeded on their trip.

Continuing through London, Ohio, Evans loaded the Harrington and Richardson revolver Tucker had bought in Ravenna. He shot three times at Roy Wilson's filling station at Wilson's Corner on Route 42, putting one of the gas pumps out of commission and puncturing the fender of Wilson's car, which was parked near the station. Then he fired a shot through a window in the Gardner Bee House as they passed, and fired another bullet through a transom in the Barnhart Oil building. Residents told Sheriff Roy Bidwell that they heard the shooting about 2:00 a.m.

By now Tucker and Evans had been on the road about sixteen hours. They were still two hours from their Cincinnati homes in their stolen Buick sedan, but it was now overheating badly, and at three in the morning they encountered the lights of the Rainbow Inn.

On U.S. 42, just west of Cedarville, the Rainbow Inn was described by a longtime resident of the hamlet as being, "Sort of down in the bottom. The place had a building where an occasional boxing match took place." Open twenty-four hours a day, the restaurant and gas station attracted local families, neighborhood farmers, tourists, and truckers traveling U.S. Route 42.

Upon entering the premises, neither Tucker nor Evans did much to call attention to themselves. Charles Douglass James, the proprietor of the place, was used to truckers and travelers en route between Cleveland, Columbus, and Cincinnati stopping at odd hours, and he was chatting with a trucker named Johnny when the two young men arrived.

James left the counter; picked up two menus, the coffee pot, and two cups; and walked over to the booth where the two were sitting.

"Care for some coffee?" James asked.

They lit cigarettes and gave a nod. James poured their coffee and noticed, he said later, that both were dressed in bib overalls and wearing flannel shirts. Johnny, the trucker at the counter, was eating sausage and eggs, and Evans took note of his meal.

"That looks good," he said. "Bring us two of what that guy is having."

James later testified as he busied himself behind the counter, he could hear conversation between the two boys, who seemed tired and said little at first. But after eating and drinking a few cups of coffee, the pair became talkative, laughing, and boasting about shooting out warehouse and car windows, and perforating road signs with well-placed shots.

James couldn't tell if they were joking and just acting tough or whether they were serious. The pair certainly were not acting like run-of-the-mill patrons who normally frequented the restaurant. They seemed churlish and rough-mannered and didn't seem to care who knew it. They interrupted Johnny, the trucker, when he said he was concerned that the bread strike in Cincinnati might hurt his deliveries. The pair bragged that if given the chance, they could break up the strike.

"That's a pretty tall order, isn't it, for two guys to break up a strike, don'cha think?" asked James, who was surprised by their brash impudence. He was even more disturbed by the response.

The boys blustered that they would hijack a truck, and Tucker asked if there was a warehouse in Xenia that they could knock off for goods they could deliver through the strikers.

"If we have to, we'll shoot it out with them," Tucker boasted to James.

At that point, James noticed the dark butt handle of a revolver protruding from the pocket of a coat that Tucker had draped over a chair, and it made the shopkeeper wary. James didn't respond to Tucker, and the pair quieted as they picked up their coats, paid their bill, and departed. A few minutes later, they returned; their Buick, which had been running fitfully when they arrived, now wouldn't start.

Tucker and Evans loitered in the restaurant for nearly two hours, huddled together, until about 5:00 a.m. They repeatedly went out into the cold night to fidget with the balky automobile, and bought a quart of oil from James. When he poured it into the engine, James noticed the shotgun in the back seat.

About five minutes later, the Buick finally rumbled to life, and the boys drove off into the pre-dawn darkness, headed southwest on Route 42 toward Xenia. "They were really out of place," James recalled later. He watched them pull away from the station, then turned and walked straight to the telephone and lifted the phone receiver off its hook.

"What number, please?" the operator asked.

"Quick, get me the sheriff, Main 281."

Chapter 5

::

The new voice on the line responded sternly, "Sheriff's office, Anderson speaking."

Joseph Anderson, a stocky, athletic forty-three-year-old and the county's only black employee in the sheriff's department, was the night duty jailer in the county's old lockup. As turnkey and booking clerk, he wore street clothes; he wasn't given a uniform.

"This is Doug James at the Rainbow Inn in Cedarville," said the Inn's owner. He described two tough-talking boys who made threats about knocking off a warehouse. They were headed for Xenia in a green two-tone '41 Buick, James said.

"They had a couple of guns. I thought you better check them out," he concluded.

Anderson's closest help was deputy Earl Confer, a fifty-three-year-old father of three children, all at home. Earl had been born and raised in nearby Yellow Springs, Ohio, and his family was well-known in the area. They ran a dairy north of downtown Xenia that made excellent ice cream. Earl had been a deputy for five years and lived with his family in an apartment on East Main Street, which was conveniently near a place just outside of town where the deputies could intercept the car and its two suspicious occupants that the caller had described.

Anderson phoned Confer, hastily put on an overcoat, and left the jail to pick up his companion in the '41 Pontiac police cruiser. Bernice Confer, the deputy's wife of thirty-one years, awoke to find Earl slipping into his striped uniform trousers, and within minutes Anderson arrived.

As the deputies rode, they planned a strategy and debated which streets might give them the best view. They didn't have long to wait: by the time Anderson and Confer had gone the few blocks on Route 42 to the edge of town, they saw car lights pacing toward them over the rolling terrain in the distance. Anderson backed the Pontiac into Lexington Avenue, a drive that branched diagonally off Route 42, and when the car passed, they recognized it as a green late-model Buick. Anderson pulled out to follow.

Within a few blocks, the Buick ran through a red light at Columbus Avenue and Church Street. Anderson stomped on the floor switch to turn on the siren and flashing lights, rounded a curve on Columbus Avenue, and moved up alongside the Buick. A block farther, at the northwest corner of Columbus and Main Street, the Buick pulled to the curb. Anderson cut off any escape by parking the cruiser ahead of it, at a slight angle.

The cruiser's right rear fender was near the Buick driver's door, so Confer was easily able to step out from the passenger side and approach Tucker, who was driving the car. Anderson walked to the passenger side and peered at Evans through the half-closed window.

"Where you going?" Anderson asked.

"To Cincinnati," Evans responded.

"Where'd you come from?"

"We come from Cincinnati."

The tone of the response bothered Anderson. "You couldn't come from Cincinnati by going toward Cincinnati," he said. "Where did you come from?"

"We come from a little town. I don't know its name," Evans sneered.

"C'mon. You must know the name."

"I said, I don't remember it."

That was enough for Anderson. "Get out!" he ordered. After he had frisked Evans, he pushed the obstinate young man around the back of the Buick. "What's your name?" Anderson asked Evans as they lurched forward.

"My name is Jones," Evans replied.

"What's your first name?"

"Sam Jones."

By this time Confer had ordered Tucker out of the car and was frisking him. "What's your buddy's name?" Anderson asked Evans.

"Scottie."

Anderson looked to the other boy. "What's your name?" he asked. "Earl," the youth responded.

"I thought you told me his name was Scottie," Anderson said to Evans. "Let's take 'em in," he suggested to Confer. The older officer agreed, and ordered the two suspects to be split up, with one riding in the cruiser, and one in their Buick.

"No," Anderson said, "Let 'em both get in our car. Let theirs sit there. It's not hurting anything."

"Let's go, boys," Confer said as he guided Tucker to the back seat of the police cruiser.

Tucker later remembered that Evans had asked the officer for permission to shut off the lights in the Buick. He reached into the car, then suddenly whirled toward the black deputy.

Chapter 6

::

Two blocks south and about five blocks west of the corner where a sheriff's cruiser and a green Buick sat against the curb the morning of January 29, 1949, my mother Ruth was cooking breakfast for my father, Judge Frank L. Johnson. She turned off the percolator loaded with Eight O'Clock coffee. She could tell the coffee was done when the entire house smelled of coffee. That's the way my father liked it.

The five-bedroom brick house with stately colonial pillars had been built by a man who disliked his neighbor to the west, so it was devoid of windows facing the disliked neighbor. Included in the home was a study, a library, and a formal dining room with double sliding French doors and a leaded glass chandelier. The living room was adorned with antique furniture and Ruth's piano. Although the house might have been more appropriate out in the country, with landscaping that included a long, tree-shaded lane, a spacious lawn, and perhaps a horse or two leaning over a fence, this home was not in the country. It had no front yard. It sat right smack-dab next to the sidewalk.

Ruth heard the Judge coming down the grand staircase and was starting to cook his eggs when the phone rang. The Judge answered and after a short conversation entered the quiet kitchen. "There's been a shootout over at Columbus and Main," he announced. "Earl Confer's dead. Joe Anderson's been wounded and was taken out to McClellan Hospital. Two boys did the shooting, and they've been caught."

My father ate his breakfast in silence and scanned the morning *Cincinnati Enquirer*, paying particular attention to yesterday's race results and the day's entries. After breakfast he backed our '37 Chevy out of the garage in back and left for Hamilton, Ohio, where he had been assigned to serve temporarily on the Butler County bench.

Frank L. Johnson, Judge of the Greene County, Ohio, Common Pleas Court (Photo courtesy of Frank L. Johnson)

Born in 1885, my father was a well-known and popular figure in the Xenia community and throughout Greene County. His father had died, and his brother had his own family by the time my father began to practice law in Xenia around 1912, so Dad was living with and supporting his mother. In the early twenties, he sang in the church choir, at the local opera house, and at the silent movies.

In 1921, my father married Mary Ruth Hodge, and the family grew to include three children. Nancy, born in 1923, would soon develop *petit mal* seizures, characterized by periodic convulsive behavior, and she would become a paranoid-schizophrenic adult who had to be institutionalized. Their next child was yours truly, Frank Lee Johnson, Jr., born in 1927. Dad nicknamed me Sonny.

Our little sister, Molly, was born in 1929. She eventually married an electrical engineer, had four children, and lives with her husband in New Jersey.

My father was an expert at pool and billiards and loved to play high-stakes poker and euchre. When he played poker, he let others believe he was superstitious. He was known to walk around his chair three times to bring himself good luck. One evening, he went out to play poker wearing an old shirt with one sleeve torn at the shoulder. He ripped the seams further, until only a few threads held the sleeve in place, and put on his suit coat. Then, after losing a few hands at the table, he stopped. "I'm losing because of this damned shirt!" he proclaimed, and with that he stood up and, to the bewilderment of his table companions, tore his shirt sleeve out of the arm of his suit coat. Whereupon, he seated himself and continued the game.

He loved little practical jokes. After dinner one night, Mother asked for part of an additional cup of coffee. Dad asked if she wanted the smallest part or the largest part of the cup filled. When she answered the smallest part, he turned the teacup upside down and filled the shallow base of the cup.

My father also bought, owned, and trained standardbred horses. He served as a starter at harness races during the county fairs. Mother also learned to love poker and horse racing, and became a reasonable handicapper. But Dad was one of the best judges of horse flesh I ever knew. He knew everything about horses, trainers, track conditions, and jockeys.

When the Great Depression came along, Dad knew he had to make a choice between his life around horses and his law practice. He could not do justice to both, and he had a wife and three children to support. He chose the honorable route and gave up his horses to concentrate on his law practice, but at heart he never gave up his horses. They were like a lost love.

My father's love for racing and gambling made him popular in local society. In the early '30s, during the depths of the Great Depression, he decided to run for the office of Judge of the Municipal Court. He ran against an elderly incumbent, and on a postcard mailed to the electorate, he explained his desire to be elected. The card pictured his three poor, bedraggled children on one side, and on the back were these words: "These are the three reasons I wish to be elected." He won easily. In 1938, he became the Greene County Common Pleas Judge, hearing civil and criminal county cases until his death in 1955.

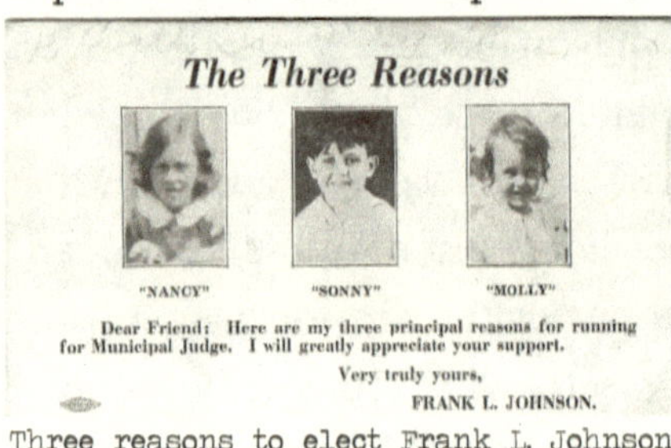

Three reasons to elect Frank L. Johnson for Judge of Xenia Municipal Court (Photo courtesy of Frank L. "Sonny" Johnson.)

In addition to his status as a judge, he was an upright citizen, literally: he was five feet, eleven inches tall, carried a modest 180 pounds on an erect frame, and was very distinguished looking with a full head of white hair.

My father loved formality. He always wore a dark blue or black suit with coat and tie, and a carnation in his lapel when they were available. During cold winter months, he wore gray woolen spats over polished black shoes. He ate breakfast, lunch, and dinner in his coat and tie. To get away from the cares of the day, he would go each evening to the Elks Club a few blocks east of our home to play cards with his friends.

That cold January morning, during his forty-five-minute drive to Butler County, he no doubt mulled the loss of his friend Earl Confer, husband of Bernice and father of three children. And Joe Anderson was hurt too, maybe badly. The Judge knew he would have to hear a murder case. It was an unpleasant thought.

: :

Earl Tucker had plenty of his own reasons to feel uncomfortable that morning. From the scene of the shooting, Sgt. Stephens had taken Tucker, handcuffed, directly to the Greene County Jail. He was searched, relieved of his belt, shoestrings, and the contents of his pockets, and pushed into a holding cell, where he would have tripped over a door sill and fallen if not for the quick hands of Denver and Charles Palmer, brothers who had been arrested, drunk, the evening before. The other resident of the holding cell that morning was John Stith, a railroad worker arrested two hours earlier for driving while intoxicated on Drake Street in Xenia. He was, by coincidence, a resident of 1973 Sutter Avenue, about a block from Ernie Evans's home in the Cincinnati suburb of English Woods.

Within minutes, Tucker's contorted posture, with hands cuffed behind his back, made the new prisoner quite uncomfortable. He complained, but officers told him in a profanity-laced retort that no one in the building had keys to unlock the cuffs. After some time passed—Tucker guessed hours—two police officers arrived to open the door of the cell and dragged him to an office, where his hands were freed, and he was again searched. Then Tucker was taken to another side of the building, isolated from others, and thrown into a harsh box he later remembered as little more than six feet deep, five feet wide, and devoid of running water, toilet facilities, or lighting. Its walls were riveted-iron sheets; its door was a lattice-work of thick iron slats. There was a board to sleep on, but no mattress. He had not slept for twenty-four hours.

The Greene County Jail building, where Earl Tucker was held, had been built before the Civil War. (Photo courtesy of Greene County Sheriff's Office.)

Ernie Evans, meanwhile, was on a hospital mattress in considerable distress. Earlier in the morning, he was writhing in pain in the middle of Columbus Avenue when the Neeld ambulance, a hearse-like vehicle with a siren and flashing light but no medical equipment, arrived to take him first to McClellan Hospital in Xenia for first aid, then to Miami Valley Hospital in Dayton, in those days a fifteen-mile, half-hour ride over a winding road. Patrolman John King rode along to guard Evans.

Upon reaching the Dayton hospital, Evans was examined and treated for a bullet wound. Probably, he was X-rayed to locate the bullet that had entered the right side of his waist just above the hip bone and which traveled in a downward position, lodging in the lower abdomen. Then, he was wheeled to a room under guard of Dayton Police Patrolman George Anderson, who had relieved Xenia's Officer King. Anderson phoned the Greene County Prosecuting Attorney Marcus Shoup to alert him that Evans was available for questioning, and Shoup promptly drove from Xenia to Dayton.

When he arrived at the hospital, Shoup found that the trip was a wasted effort. Evans was in no condition to be questioned. Doctors had administered anesthesia, and they began surgery on the prisoner at 1:00 p.m. After a two-hour operation, during which they removed several inches of Evans's small intestines, he was pronounced in "serious" condition. Shoup, meanwhile, had to return to Xenia without answers as to why one of the county's deputies had been killed.

: :

For the time being, Clarence Earl Tucker was the only participant in the shooting death of Deputy Earl Confer available for interrogation. Dragged from his tiny cell around noon and escorted to Sheriff Walton Spahr's office, Tucker later described his state of mind by then as "thorough confusion, befuddled and bewilderment." He sat utterly alone against a phalanx of antagonistic strangers. The two Cincinnati detectives, Mezger and Schath, stood before him, along with Deputy Sheriff Pete Mahan. Another man took notes, and one with a camera crept behind Tucker and popped a flashbulb. Mezger began by sneering that if this had happened in Cincinnati, police likely would have beaten Tucker to death.

"I'll tell you anything you need to know," Tucker responded. Schath pulled a fistful of papers from a pocket, handed them to Mezger, and began his questioning.

He listed a couple of break-ins and some burglaries that Tucker denied any knowledge of. Then Schath asked about fifteen cases of whiskey someone had stolen from Kemper Lane Hotel. Tucker admitted guilt in that caper, and told the detectives that he and Evans had sold the liquor in Newport.

"How did you transport the booze to Kentucky?" Schath asked.

"We used a car," Tucker said.

"Where did you get the car?"

"We stole it over in English Woods."

"Did you steal a car in Avondale?"

"No, sir."

Asked if the car they were driving this morning was the one stolen in Cincinnati, Tucker revealed that the pair had in fact stolen three Buicks in total, leaving the first two burning near Akron. The car he was driving this morning was a "hot" car, he admitted without recognizing the pun. "It's a piece of junk. It's missing badly," Tucker added.

"What did you buy with all that money from the whiskey?" Schath asked.

"Well, we had a good time in Newport. And we bought these red shirts," Tucker said, tugging at the clothing he was still wearing.

Schath asked where Tucker and Evans had gotten the gun that had been used in the shooting that morning, and Tucker answered he had used almost the last of his whiskey money to buy it in Ravenna. Mezger interrupted to ask about the shotgun in the car, and Tucker explained that it belonged to his grandfather, and that he had never used it.

Mezger and Schath had heard everything they needed to know, so they abruptly ended the questioning, and Tucker was thrown back into his iron box. Eventually he was served lunch, a gruel with dirty, extinguished cigarette butts sticking out of it. Tucker complained, but this was to be common fare. For the ten weeks he was incarcerated in the Xenia jail, breakfast consisted of a small bowl of cornflakes with skim milk. For lunch and dinner, he received about a cupful of macaroni "and some kind of tails curled in there, maybe two of those tails," Tucker remembered. "I'd find cigarette butts, cigarettes, matches in it. When I complained, they would take it around the corner, take the butt out, and bring it back."

Uniformed deputies visited the cell about an hour after he ate, gruffly demanded that Tucker identify himself, and repeated questions about the shooting. Late in the afternoon, he was again yanked from his cell and taken across the street to the city jail to be interrogated by Oznl H. Cornwell, Superintendent of Ohio's Bureau of Identification and Investigation, and Prosecutor Shoup.

Cornwell had been the Xenia Chief of Police before accepting his position with the state. In the 1930s, the Cornwells, along with Sheriff Walton Spahr's family, lived a few houses from my family. Richard Cornwell, the former chief's son, was about my age. I remember Richard telling me while we were playing that he wanted to be a gangster when he grew up. I do not know if he made it or not. The family moved to London, Ohio, in 1940 after the Colonel accepted the Superintendent's post.

Marcus Shoup, Greene County Prosecutor, in 1946 (Photo courtesy of Greene County Public Library Greene Room -- Local History and Genealogy, Xenia, Ohio)

As an attorney and prosecutor, Marcus Shoup was ambitious, determined, and zealous, as well as artistic and passionate. Born in 1902 and the father of eight children at the time of the Xenia shootings, Shoup was an accomplished violinist who had studied the instrument in New York City under the master and teacher, Ovide Musin. Finally realizing that as a violinist he lacked the greatness of a master, he turned to law and politics. Marcus's wife, Dorothy, had studied piano at the Cincinnati Conservatory of Music, and both of them played in the symphony orchestra of Springfield, a medium-sized city just north of Xenia.

Shoup became head of the Republican Party in Greene County. My father and mother would entertain officials of the Party in their home. After dinner, Marcus and Dorothy would entertain the guests with Dvorak, Beethoven, and energetic Slavic tunes. I would sit atop the stairs and listen to the music until well past my bedtime.

My father, the Judge, would tell friends stories about Shoup. In one, they were together in Columbus, Ohio, for a state Republican Convention before hotels had air conditioning. Their room was on the fourth floor; it was summer and the windows were open. As Shoup played passionate Gypsy-influenced music on his violin, the Judge went to a window to get some fresh air. He looked down to the street and saw about fifty people on the sidewalk listening to the free concert.

My father was fond of other Shoup stories. According to one tale, Shoup frequently visited his aunt, who owned a parrot that was kept in the kitchen. Visitors who entered the house passed through the kitchen door, and every time Shoup passed the parrot, he repeated the same sentence. Soon the parrot learned the exact phrase, "Democrats are dirty bastards," and repeated it for anyone and everyone.

Shoup may have aspired to higher office. He certainly wanted to win this case against these two "dirty bastards," hoodlums who had come into his county and snuffed out the life of a Greene County deputy he knew well. But quickly, it became apparent that while the State could build a solid case against Evans, no one had seen

Tucker do anything except stand aside and watch the scene unfold. To convict him, too, the prosecutor would have to link him to the crime.

So, late in the afternoon of January 29, Clarence Earl Tucker faced a room full of law enforcement officials primed for interrogation. Shoup and Cornwell joined Fred Dengler (Cornwell's chief investigator and a gun expert), Sheriff Walton Spahr, and Spahr's son, Deputy Lee Spahr. Mostly, these others glared at the prisoner as Shoup and especially Cornwell asked questions. Cornwell began, suggesting that Tucker make a statement describing the events that led to the shooting incident, and Tucker agreed. Shoup sent for the county stenographer, Ms. Dorothy McFadden, while Tucker recalled his childhood friendship with Evans, their theft of liquor from the Kemper Lane Hotel, and their subsequent road trip to Northeast Ohio. Tucker admitted the theft of the two Buicks in Cleveland and described the purchase of the revolver.

About this time, stenographer Dorothy McFadden joined the group. She was a stout woman with a well-deserved reputation for taking excellent shorthand, a skill she needed as Shoup and Cornwell took positions on either side of the prisoner and began to pepper him with statements about the shooting. "I was thoroughly confused," Tucker recalled later, "but the two asking questions at the same time made the matter worse."

Cornwell began. "Why did you buy that gun?"

"It was foolishness. The whole trip was foolishness," Tucker replied.

"So why did you have it on the front seat of the car?" Cornwell asked. Shoup jumped in.

"You had the gun to use?"

"I thought it was a deal."

"The guy in the restaurant said you had it with you then," said Cornwell, inches from Tucker's face. "So why did you carry the revolver with you every time you got out of the car?"

"I dunno."

Cornwell asked about the shotgun in the car, and Tucker said it was an old thing that had been in the family for years. His grandfather had sawed it off, and it wouldn't shoot very far, he said, and in fact he had never shot it at all.

"Why did you have it loaded?" Cornwell shouted.

"We was in a hot car," Tucker said, "and we thought we might hang out of the window and shoot at people chasing us, maybe pepper their windshield to scare 'em off."

"In other words," Cornwell continued, "you discussed that angle with Evans, and he discussed that with you, that wording, 'shoot it out' if necessary, is that right?"

"We just made that agreement once, about using the shotgun, that's all."

"Well, did you have any conversation or understanding with Ernest that if anybody tried to stop you, you had the gun and would use it, and you had it for that purpose?" Cornwell pushed.

"We started conversations like that, but we never finished them all the way, what we would do," Tucker insisted again.

"When did you have this understanding with the two of you in connection with this gun that if anybody tried to stop you, you were going to shoot it out with them and not get caught?"

"That was in Cincinnati when we had the shotgun," Tucker said.

Shoup was clearly agitated. "What about the revolver?" he yelled. "You had the gun for the purpose if somebody was going to stop you?"

"No."

"Cross that out, Dorothy."

"You know what a conspiracy is, don't you?" Shoup asked, nearly shouting.

"Yes."

"So you and Evans were in a conspiracy to shoot it out with police!"

"No."

"Scratch that out!"

The interrogation continued in this fashion for some time—Tucker later guessed more than an hour—with Shoup and Cornwell repeatedly firing questions simultaneously. They demanded that Tucker admit a pact, and in their attempts to coerce Tucker into signing a confession to that effect, Tucker was always queried in the same way: "You and Evans made a pact between the two of you, that if caught, you would shoot your way out and not be taken alive, didn't you?" Tucker would answer "No," and the prosecutor would have the stenographer scratch out the answer. Then the question would be asked again, in the same yes or no fashion, in an attempt to get Tucker to admit to a conspiracy. He would not and never did. He remained adamant throughout his life that there was no death pact between himself and Evans.

The interrogators didn't physically abuse Tucker, but he remembered his treatment as harsh during the next fourteen days. Every few hours, different uniformed officers came to his cell to question him. Most of the time, he was so exhausted he had no idea who the men were or who they represented. Alone, frightened, and with only a ninth-grade education, he was willing to tell officials anything they wanted to know, and he testified later that "he was afraid to ask for anything, including an attorney."

By Wednesday morning, Tucker's adamant refusal to admit to collusion left Shoup with a problem of direction. He met first with Xenia Police Chief Stanley Nickell, in whose jurisdiction the murder had occurred, and with Officers King and Stephens, who had responded to the scene of the incident. Then he interviewed witnesses Isaiah Rose, Lawrence Byrd, and Marcus Walker. Chief Nickell, meanwhile, visited Deputy Joe Anderson, who was being treated for his leg wound in Xenia's McClellan Hospital. The bullet fired by Evans had been removed about noon Tuesday, and Anderson was comfortable enough to speak. (Within a few weeks, however, the injury would bother Anderson enough he would require surgery at Cincinnati's Good Samaritan Hospital for a damaged sciatic nerve.)

Late Wednesday morning, a uniformed deputy sheriff retrieved Tucker from his cell and led him through the jail building to a small office near the street. Marcus Shoup sat in the room with Mrs. McFadden, and Tucker was placed in a chair with his back to the door.

"Where were you born?" Shoup asked.

"A little town in eastern Oregon," Tucker answered.

"I see in your records you went to a couple of schools in Cincinnati. Is that true, Clarence?"

"Yes."

"Why did you change schools?" Shoup continued further into Tucker's life in Cincinnati, then changed direction to ask about the kinds of things the two boys had done on their trip to the Akron area. "It was on the way back that this shooting occurred, right?"

"Yes, sir."

Suddenly Shoup jumped up, pointed at Tucker, looked up, and shouted. "There!" Shoup yelled. "You heard him yourself! He confessed!"

Tucker turned around. In the doorway stood a deputy with Tucker's uncle Neal. The two relatives were barely able to exchange a glance before the officer pulled Neal away, and Clarence was pushed back to his cell.

Neal was the only Tucker family member able to take time from work to visit the young relative in jail in the days after the shooting, but Tucker's grandmother, Ella, had been the first in the family to hear the news. Before noon Tuesday morning, a Cincinnati radio announcer said Clarence Earl Tucker and his friend Ernest Finley Evans had been arrested for the murder of a Xenia deputy. Hysterical, she ran upstairs screaming and crying to Earl's father, Popeye, who had to quiet her before she could tell him the horrible news. Popeye telephoned his father, Claude, and brother, Neal, but the trio agreed that because they had to work they would not be able to get away until the next day, when Neal could drive to Xenia to see if they could visit his nephew and get more details of the crime.

The reporters came a few hours later. Ella told them Earl and Ernie had been friends for years and had seen each other a lot since Evans was discharged from the Army the previous October. Her grandson was exempt from service because polio had affected his left leg, she added.

Inquiring reporters first broke the news to Mrs. Alice Evans. Told on her doorstep that her Ernie was in a Dayton, Ohio, hospital in serious condition with a bullet wound, and that he was a suspect in the murder of a police officer, she promptly collapsed in a faint. When she was revived, Alice talked about Ernie's good record in the Army, and she said that he even had been an aviation cadet. Since his discharge, he had once again been hanging around with Tucker, but her son's old friend made her uneasy. "Every time those two get together, they get into trouble," she said.

Chapter 7

::

The reporters who queried Alice Evans were chasing a big story for newspapers in both Cincinnati and Xenia. Cincinnati's *Enquirer*, *Times-Star*, and *Post* all printed page-one stories that emphasized the backgrounds of the local boys arrested for the crime. In Xenia, the story dominated the front page of *The Evening Gazette*, a Monday-through-Saturday daily. Normally, its eight pages included local, national, and foreign news; an opinion page; and a page on the business world, with coverage of grain and selected stock market prices. Another page covered local club news and recognized wedding anniversaries and the sick; a couple of pages were devoted to classified ads, and a page printed the daily "funnies." The paper was printed by 2:30 p.m. and distributed to its readers around 3:30 p.m., after the delivery boys got out of school.

On the afternoon of Tuesday, January 29, the front-page headline of *The Evening Gazette* blared:

SHERIFF'S DEPUTY KILLED IN GUNFIGHT ON XENIA STREET

Earl Confer Slain;
2nd Local Officer and Youth Wounded

The accompanying text stated in detail that the prosecutor questioned the pair about the blaze of gunfire that killed the deputy and that the chief of police, Stanley Nickell, was in charge of the investigation.

Photos published with the article showed Evans in his Army Air Corps uniform, complete with necktie and his hat cocked to one side. He appeared slender and good looking, clean-shaven with dark hair, thick eyebrows and bright, friendly eyes. His girl-winning, choir-boy smile radiated confidence. Tucker, on the other hand, was known only from police mug photos. With a mop of scruffy hair, half-open droopy eyes, and an unkempt, sullen appearance, he looked the part of a killer. It was an image at odds with all the newspaper accounts, which related police reports that throughout the gun duel, Tucker stood by meekly, with his back to the action and "his hands in the air, crying, 'Don't shoot again,'" as *The Cincinnati Enquirer* reported.

: :

Although Greene County's offices closed as usual Wednesday afternoon, Marcus Shoup kept busy. After having no doubt listened carefully to the two Cincinnati detectives and Cornwell on the day of the crime, he met again with Chief Nickell and Sheriff Spahr. They could easily cite the Ohio Criminal Code in the shooting death: "whoever purposely and willfully kills a . . . deputy sheriff . . . while said . . . deputy sheriff . . . is in discharge of his duties, is guilty of murder in the first degree and shall be punished by death." In addition, they knew the precedent set by a case, Ralls v. State, in which a defendant's confession, corroborated by evidence, had established a conspiracy that was used to convict all the defendants linked to the murder of an Ohio county sheriff. Shoup called reporters to his office before their late-morning deadline and announced formal charges in the case would be filed the next day. Evans, Shoup said, would be charged with first-degree murder; charges against Tucker were undecided.

The Greene County Commissioners made an announcement at noon as well. All county offices would close from 2:00 to 3:00 p.m. Thursday, during the funeral of Deputy Sheriff Earl Confer at Neeld Funeral Home in Xenia. Wednesday evening, Confer's widow, daughter, and two sons, as well as his father, two brothers, and three sisters, received friends and well-wishers at the funeral parlor.

Deputy Earl Confer (Photo courtesy Wright State University, *Dayton Daily News* Archives)

By Thursday morning, Shoup had made up his mind. Formal affidavits charging first-degree murder were filed, the language of the documents saying that both Ernest Finley Evans and Clarence Earl Tucker had killed Deputy Confer while he was performing his duties as a law officer. Tucker would be brought into Greene County Common Pleas Court and arraigned soon. Evans's condition would not allow him to be present when he was to be formally charged, and Shoup told reporters that Evans might not be arraigned before the county grand jury could be assembled to consider the indictments against the two youths. Then, the county offices were shuttered to honor the memory of Earl Confer.

Several hundred people filled Neeld Funeral Home for Deputy Confer's funeral at 2:00 p.m. The Reverend J. W. Wedgewood of Xenia's Trinity Methodist Church officiated. Following the eulogies, a trio of Ohio State Highway Patrol cruisers escorted the funeral procession on U.S. Route 42 en route to Spring Valley Cemetery, about eight miles south of town, while the city's police halted traffic at major intersections. Deputy Confer was a native of Yellow Springs, a village north of Xenia, and in his obituary published that day in the community's weekly newspaper, a bewildered *Yellow Springs News*, could only comment, "as in all cases like this, there are many rumors."

The next day, Xenia Police Chief Stanley Nickell, Sheriff Walton Spahr, and Prosecutor Marcus Shoup drove to Dayton for their first opportunity to question Evans. Because of Evans's temperament and condition, it's very doubtful that he divulged much. Indeed, he may have remembered little about the incident. He probably squirmed in discomfort from his trauma and possibly was under sedation. In 1946, the new antibiotic penicillin was not particularly effective on intestinal bacteria, so before his incision was closed, doctors probably dusted the abdominal cavity with sulfanilamide powder, commonly used in World War II to combat gangrene and to prevent infections. Whether or not the sulfa was used, after surgery Evans developed severe peritonitis.

Nothing Shoup, Spahr, and Nickell heard from Evans changed the prosecutor's thinking. Upon his return to Xenia, Shoup prepared indictment documents against the two boys, stating in them that on the twenty-ninth of January, 1946, Ernest Finley Evans and Clarence Earl Tucker had "purposefully and willfully" killed Earl Confer, "while said Earl Confer was in the discharge of his duties as said Deputy Sheriff of said County of Greene." To emphasize the point, Shoup had the exact citation number, "G.C. 12402-1," typed in as an insertion into the pre-printed general statement, "Contrary to the statute in such case made and provided, and against the peace and dignity of the state of Ohio" on the indictment form.

Because my father, Judge Johnson, was serving temporarily on the bench in Butler County during the week, Shoup hadn't yet conferred with him about the case. The two met at the end of the week, with Saturday's *Evening Gazette* reporting that Judge Johnson would call a special January session of the grand jury the following Thursday to consider first-degree murder charges against the pair. Over the weekend, Tucker and Evans were served with the notice of their indictments.

Tucker's family learned that Earl likely would be the target of murder charges when his father, Popeye, tried to visit on Friday afternoon and was rebuffed. Recognizing the need for legal assistance, Popeye and Neal contacted a well-known Cincinnati lawyer, William F. "Foss" Hopkins, early in the week after Tucker was served with the indictment papers. At mid-week, Neal met with Hopkins, who laid out a strategy for defending Tucker. To begin the process, Hopkins sent a telegraphed message to Tucker in his cell, urging the defendant to plead not guilty in his upcoming arraignment and recommending that Tucker decline any offer for court-appointed legal assistance.

Unfortunately for Tucker, a court-appointed attorney would work for free, but Hopkins would not. He wanted $1,500 to continue the defense, a sum the working-class Tucker family was unable to accumulate. "We was undecided what to do," Popeye recalled later. "We couldn't raise the money at that time."

As a result at his arraignment on Monday, February 11, Tucker stood alone before Judge Johnson. He took Foss Hopkins's advice, pleading "not guilty," and the Judge announced there could be no bond because this was a murder case. Then he asked Tucker about his lack of defense counsel. "We'll see what we can do about that," the Judge responded when Tucker said he had no representation.

Judge Johnson then ordered a pool of sixty citizens to be drawn for the trial and set the trial date for April 1. Normally, jury pools consisted of around forty prospects, but the Judge apparently felt a larger pool was needed to seat an unbiased jury. With that done, he adjourned the court, the calendar now taking priority.

The time had come for a three-week vacation he had scheduled. Because automobile production had been suspended from 1941 until 1946, the Judge and Ruth had been driving their 1937 Chevy for way too long. David Purdom, of Purdom Motor Sales, had promised the Judge that he would become the owner of the first new Plymouth the dealership received, and the car had arrived. So, the Judge and Ruth drove their gleaming maroon '46

Plymouth to Miami, Florida to attend the horse races, but letters I received indicated they did not have much luck at Hialeah that year.

: :

Wednesday morning, February 12, local attorney E. Dawson Smith appeared at Tucker's cell door. A former Xenia municipal court judge, Dawson Smith had been asked by Judge Johnson to represent Tucker. His nephew, George H. Smith, who had sat on the Common Pleas bench prior to my father, would assist. The attorney and his new client spoke for a few minutes, with Tucker relating what had happened, and Smith explaining that community outrage at the killing would make the case difficult. However, the attorneys were confident they could win an acquittal for Tucker, Smith said.

Tucker's confinement loosened a bit after his arraignment. Years later, he recalled that although he was still in solitary confinement, his jailers began to unlock the cell door at dawn, and again in the evening before dark, allowing Tucker to move around that part of the jail building. The food improved, too: he could supplement his jail rations with milk, rolls, or pie.

His captors also began to allow family visits. After Neal's brief appearance the morning after the shooting, Popeye tried to visit two days later; then his brothers drove to Xenia on Wednesday before Tucker's arraignment. A few days later, Popeye's wife, Mary, went to the jail. All were rebuffed by sarcastic jailers. "You seem like such nice folks," the police would say. "How come the boy went bad?"

After the arraignment, however, the Smiths arranged for Popeye and Neal to talk with Tucker, although when the brothers appeared, the captors insisted that one or more deputies sit with the group during the visit. Discussions were closely monitored, with no mention of Earl's court case allowed. Once, while Deputy Pete Mahan was eavesdropping, Mary, Popeye's wife, inadvertently mentioned the upcoming court trial. Mahan promptly interrupted the conversation and hustled Popeye and Mary out of the jail.

During this period, the Smiths brought news that their case had become more complicated. In early March, Ernie Evans was transferred from the hospital in Dayton to the Greene County Infirmary. Evans was listed in "fair" condition while he stayed in this significant two-story brick institution about two miles outside of Xenia on the Dayton-Xenia road. *The Evening Gazette* indicated that he was "slowly recovering" from his wound and had already cost the citizens of Greene county $1,809.35, according to figures released by Shoup. But clearly Evans was able to meet with the Smiths, because on March 7, the court-appointed counsels Smith and Smith filed an entry with the Common Pleas Court, declaring that the two defendants in the case were indigent and unable to employ counsel. My father, having just returned from Florida, then officially appointed the Smiths to represent Tucker and Evans. He hinted that because of the poor condition of the defendant, the trial might be postponed from its original April 1 target date.

Legal strategies for both the defense and the prosecution began to take shape quickly from this point. In mid-March, Evans was moved to a cot in the county jail, where he was arraigned and entered a plea of "not guilty." Two days later, on March 19, Marcus Shoup filed an application to have the two young men tried jointly, arguing that the defendants had committed the crime in concert, "the act of one being the act of the other." In court papers, he suggested that the evidence to be presented at a joint trial would be identical, regardless of whether there would be one or two trials, and he noted that a joint trial would enable the jury to weigh testimony and evidence as it affected each defendant. Judge Johnson granted the request.

The Smiths countered by advising Evans and Tucker to waive their right to a jury and instead have the case heard before a judge. Years later, Tucker recalled that the Smiths warned of the hostile environment in the county, which would make it difficult to impanel a jury that would return a favorable or even a just verdict. *The Evening Gazette* was publishing frequent front-page stories that reminded readers of the crime, and in Cedarville, the hamlet where Evans and Tucker had stopped for breakfast, the weekly *Cedarville Herald* blatantly referred to the pair as "two Cincinnati thugs." In addition, the Smiths had to be cognizant of tactics that would be tried by a prosecutor in a murder trial. Shoup would drag a weeping widow to the witness stand and then have the coroner describe, in gory detail, the death and autopsy findings. A jury would be greatly influenced by this type of testimony. On the other hand, a judge, knowing the tricks of a prosecutor, would be less impressed and less influenced by emotional testimony.

Friday, March 22, the Smiths filed the waiver request, signed by both Evans and Tucker. The following Tuesday, Judge Johnson announced his approval, adding that he had asked Chief Justice Carl V. Weygandt of the Ohio Supreme Court to assign two other judges to sit with him in a three-judge panel that would be convened April 23 for the first-degree murder trial of the two indicted Cincinnati youths.

It would be an historic first: a tribunal had never been formed to hear a capital case in Greene County. The Judge didn't know who would be assigned, he told the newspaper, and it was possible neither he nor the other two judges would know who would serve until the day of the trial. However, by the time the trial began, the other jurists were known: Judge Harry M. Rankin of Washington Court House, a farming community of Xenia's size about forty miles southeast of Xenia, and Alton F. Brown of Lebanon, the historic small town that featured the Golden Lamb Inn on Route 42 midway between Dayton and Cincinnati. My father would serve as presiding judge. All three jurists knew each other; they had been friends for many years.

My father must have felt pangs of dilemma at this point in preparations for the trial. He did not want to alienate his friend, Prosecutor Marcus Shoup, nor a city whose citizens were demanding justice, and who had elected him. The Judge chose to have the case heard in Greene County.

Why not order a change of venue? Probably my father felt that if he could hold the trial under his own jurisdiction, this might be the best chance for a plea of leniency to be heard. Correspondence between myself and my parents at the time clearly indicates my father's concern for the two boys.

My mother wrote the following in an undated letter written shortly after the shootout: "Dad has to hear the murder case of the two boys who shot our deputy sheriff. It is a very unpleasant task for Dad, because they are so young and he feels so sorry for them. Having a boy of our own so far away from home makes us worry more, I guess. Every night we ask God to take good care of you and bring you safely back to us as soon as possible."

In a letter I sent to my parents dated April 5, 1946, I responded:

> *Don't worry about my disposition changing. I haven't changed a bit. It just seems that I have grown up so quickly. I am sorry to hear that Dad has to hear the two boys' case but don't worry about me. I'll never come home like they are. Don't worry about me.*
>
> *~Sonny*

Chapter 8

::

My father left our home the morning of April 23, 1946, and walked to the courthouse in a somber mood. It was a warm spring day with a predicted high in the 60s and a threat of rain, and although lilacs were in bloom and he loved their fragrant aroma, he hardly noticed them as he passed by manicured lawns. He loved to whistle, but today he wasn't whistling. His mind was on the upcoming murder trial, and he had to arrive at his chambers before the two visiting judges got to his office. He had to remember to stash away the hatchet he kept under his desk. Although he never intended to use it, he kept the hatchet there in case some disgruntled past offender came to his chambers and threatened him. He vowed he would pick up his hatchet and tell the person to, in no uncertain words, "get the hell out of my office."

At the same time my father was strolling toward the courthouse, two attendants from the county infirmary, or the "poor house" as it was called locally, were arriving in white starched uniforms at the county jail to help Evans shower, shave, and dress. By strict orders from the defense team, both he and Tucker were to appear in the courtroom wearing dark suits, white shirts, and neckties. Counsel felt strongly that a defendant in a courtroom could never be presumed innocent while wearing jailhouse garb that displayed stenciling on the shirt and stripes on the trousers.

Around 8:15 a.m., Evans and his attendants joined an entourage leaving the jail for the courthouse. Sheriff Spahr led the procession, followed by Evans in a wheelchair and an infirmary attendant pushing the chair. Alice Evans walked beside her son. Two armed men in uniforms followed the starched attendants; next came Tucker, whose polio-weakened leg slowed his gait, and his father Popeye. Two more armed guards walked behind them, and Claude and Neal Tucker brought up the rear.

The group's slow progress took the defendants past the inviting lawns, huge shade trees, and sidewalk benches that surrounded the Greene County Courthouse. Built in 1902 by traveling stonecutters from hand-cut blocks of locally quarried, prison-gray limestone, the edifice was, and still is, crowned by its bell tower with a town clock atop a bright red, tiled roof visible not only from all sides but for several miles outside the city. The architecture has questionable heritage: it has been described as a combination of styles, with touches of Gothic. A giant cannon of naval origin was at some point mounted on the southwest corner of the square, facing the Corner Pharmacy. The drug store, which sat diagonally on the opposite corner, would have been blown to kingdom come if the inoperable gun had been fired. After the Xenia tornado of 1974, the cannon was moved to the north side of the courthouse and now threatens the city building, should the city ever attempt to secede from the county.

When the prisoners and their group reached the Detroit Street entrance to the courthouse, the two male attendants lifted the wheelchair. One of four entrances to the County Court building in 1946, the pair of massive oak doors facing Detroit Street gave admission past winged lions on each side. Except for the west side interior, dominated by a split marble staircase leading to the second floor, the building to this day features high ceilings and cavernous, marble-floored atriums leading to county offices.

That April morning, prospective gallery attendees swarmed over the lawn, staring and whispering as the group made its way toward the courthouse doors. Farmers, dressed in their best flannel—buttoned at the neck, formal-like—and nearly new bib overalls—both straps up, and fastened—had come to town specifically to take in the show. A couple of them politely disposed of their wads of "Red Man" chew before entering the building. In the courtroom, some of the town's semi-retired attorneys sat in a group in the back of the gallery and chatted amongst themselves. The Confer and Anderson families entered, as did a weeping Alice Evans, as well as Tucker's father and grandfather. The gallery was filled by 8:30 a.m.

By the time my father entered the courthouse at 8:10 a.m., the gallery was beginning to fill. The other two judges, Rankin and Brown, arrived by 8:30 a.m., and the three old friends exchanged small talk for a few minutes. Then Bailiff Hamilton quietly rapped on the door to Judge Johnson's chambers.

"Judge, the gallery is completely full, and we're wondering, since the jury box isn't going to be used, would it be possible to allow spectators to sit in the jury box?"

Judge Johnson turned to the other two judges, who nodded their approval. "It's okay with us, as long as it is done in an orderly and dignified manner," the Judge said. "But if anybody gets demonstrative or disorderly, we'll order them removed."

With that said, the bailiff allowed spectators to fill the jury box. The trial of the State of Ohio v. Clarence Earl Tucker and Ernest Finley Evans was about to begin. The spectators filling the outer hallway were turned away.

One of those waiting out in the hallway was June Marie Edwards. She had been stunned in mid-March when two deputies from Greene County arrived, summons in hand, at the Edwards' home in Freedom. She hadn't heard a word from Ernie Evans since the last time she saw him on Saturday, January 26, and the news the deputies brought left her sobbing in disbelief. She couldn't understand what had happened to Ernie, and besides, her state cosmetology board exams were upcoming. But her father explained that the law required that she go to testify, so he and June accompanied Minard's store clerk Wayne Porter, who also had received a summons, on the 200-mile trip down to Xenia.

"I had never seen a courtroom in my life," June remembered. "We sat in chairs at the top of the long flight of steps. They brought Ernie up, and I was so shocked that I collapsed. When I came to, my dad was talking to me, telling me to calm down."

June was stunned because Evans clearly was not well. His peritonitis had improved, but he had lost about twenty pounds and now weighed a little over 145 pounds. What had once been bright blue eyes now lacked luster. As his attendants carried him up the long flight of stairs to the courtroom level, jail physician Dr. R. L. Haines and his nurse, Winifred Stuckey, both from the rural village of Jamestown, east of Xenia, followed close behind.

Spectators entering the courtroom found seats in the gallery on both sides of a center aisle, on unpadded oak benches that resembled pews in a church. An oak railing with a swinging gate in its center separated the gallery from the main portion of the room. The elevated bench for the judges was directly ahead in the center of the far wall. To the left of the bench, a large stained glass window displayed a blindfolded justice in her flowing white gown, holding a balance scales. Lettering scrolled around the glass proclaims, "The Law Delights in Equity. It Loves Perfection. It is a Rule of Right." Across the bottom of the glass it reads, "The Safety Of The People Is The Supreme Law."

Upon entering, Evans, Tucker, and the defense counsel were surprised to find the jury box along the left wall filled with spectators. The defense table and chairs were to the left of the gate and the prosecutors to the right. Ashtrays sat on both tables, and a couple of spittoons were strategically situated on the floor nearby. Court stenographer Dorothy McFadden sat directly in front of the judges' bench, holding her stenographer's pad and sharpened pencils ready to write the testimony in shorthand. The witness stand was to the left of the gallery and immediately to the right of the bench.

"Hear Ye, Hear Ye!" the bailiff announced. "The Common Pleas Court in the County of Greene will now be in session with the Honorable Judge Frank L. Johnson presiding. All who are able, please rise." All but one, Evans, stood at attention while the three black-robed judges entered the courtroom and proceeded to the elevated bench, where Judge Johnson pounded his gavel on the bar and announced, "You may be seated." The boys had been instructed to sit upright in their chairs, be silent, and look directly at the bench during the entire hearing. They were told to do nothing that would turn the court against them. "If there is too much strain caused by looking at the bench then lower your eyes and head slightly," they were told.

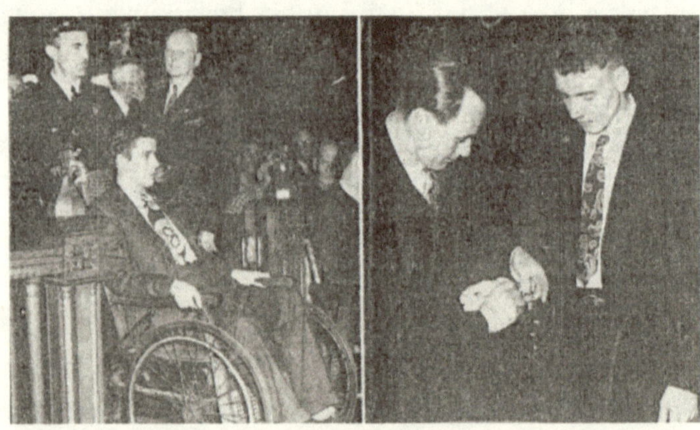

Photos from contemporary newspaper account show Evans in wheelchair and Tucker being released from handcuffs. (Newspaper clip courtesy of Wright State University, *Dayton Daily News* Archives)

Marcus Shoup made the first request of the three judges, a tour to the scene of the crime about three blocks away. The judges agreed, and rose with the prosecutors and the defense attorneys to go to the scene. Hardly any of the gallery left their seats while the court officials were gone, although a few slipped out to have a smoke or a chew. Most were afraid to leave the room for fear they would lose their seats.

The judges returned by mid-morning. When they were settled, they heard Prosecutor Shoup outline the escapades of the youths from the time they robbed a Cincinnati hotel of several cases of whiskey, drove a stolen car to the Cleveland and Akron areas, and became involved in two more auto thefts prior to their arrival in Xenia.

George Smith, on the other hand, waived an opening statement for his two clients. Rather, he asked the court for a recess so that Evans' wound could be attended to. A short recess was declared, and the young man was wheeled into the judge's chamber, which contained a lavatory where Nurse Stuckey and Dr. Haines gave medical attention to the draining bullet wound in Evans' right side.

The recess over, County Coroner Dr. H.C. Schick became the first witness called to the stand by the prosecution. After the preliminary questions of who called the coroner and of the place and time of his arrival, he was asked to describe his findings.

"Upon my arrival at the scene of the shooting, I found one Earl Confer, Deputy Sheriff of Greene County, whom I recognized immediately," Dr. Schick testified. "He was lying on his back on the curb at the northwest corner of the intersection of Columbus and Main Street.

"I observed one bullet wound through the clothing, the bullet wound on the right side posteriorly," he continued, adding that in a detailed examination at Neeld Funeral Home he found that the bullet had entered the deputy's body on the right side of his chest, passed through both lungs, pierced the heart, passed through the spleen, and was found just beneath the skin outside the rib cage.

"Considering the way the bullet pierced the body of Earl Confer," Shoup questioned, "would death probably be sudden?"

"I would say from all the damage, internal damage, that was done, that death occurred within a minute or two," Dr. Schick replied.

The next witnesses to testify was Sergeant Ancil Stephens, who told of finding Officer John King and Isaiah Rose with guns pointing at Tucker, Evans lying face down in the street, and the parked cars.

"Did you have a chance to examine the inside of the Buick?" asked Shoup. "If so, will you tell the court what you found?"

"Yes sir. The thing I found to be of the greatest interest was a double-barreled shotgun, fully loaded, on the floor of the back seat."

The prosecutor had photos of the Buick and the shotgun admitted to the court as evidence. He then called Patrolman King of the Xenia Police, who described the scene of the event; Bernice Confer, the widow, who identified the clothing worn by Deputy Confer on the fatal morning; and observers Lawrence Byrd, Marcus Walker, and George Sams. Isaiah Rose described his role as a temporary guard in the incident, and Doug James, who ran the restaurant outside of Cedarville, identified the two suspects and their threatening attitudes.

After a recess for lunch, the State called forward Fred P. Dengler, Chief Investigator, Gun Identification Expert, State Bureau of Criminal Identification and Investigation in London, Ohio. Denger, a ballistics expert, first identified bullets that were fired from the Harrington and Richardson gun and then did the same with the bullet fired from Confer's .38 caliber Smith and Wesson, extracted from the body of Evans. The ballistics of the bullet taken from the body of Deputy Sheriff Confer and the bullet removed from the thigh of Deputy Anderson matched the markings of bullets fired from the Harrington and Richardson. He described how test bullets were fired and compared microscopically to the bullets from the victims, detailing the similarities between the scratches—called lands and grooves—that the different bullets made. The bullets were from the weapons displayed to the court and entered into evidence in the case, he concluded.

Then, Deputy Sheriff Joseph Anderson was called before the court. Members of the gallery leaned forward to hear as Anderson, the lone black man to serve as an officer of the law in all of Greene County, including the city, described the telephone call from Cedarville, his call to Confer, and their strategy as they saw the Buick coming and backed into Lexington Avenue. He discussed the traffic stop and their initial interrogation of the two in the car. He told how the two pairs of men were about to split up when Anderson suggested they all should go in the patrol car.

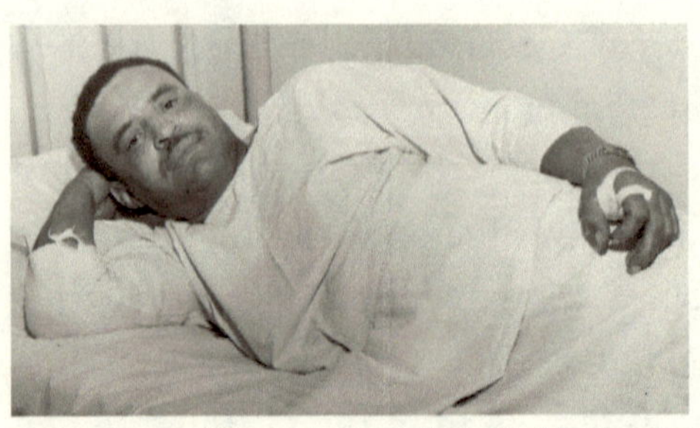
Deputy Joseph Anderson, hospitalized for the gunshot wound suffered in the Xenia shooting (Photo courtesy of Wright State University *Dayton Daily News* Archives)

"We started toward our car, and Evans whirled away from me and reached back on the seat of the Buick and came up shooting," Anderson testified. "He said, 'Get them up, you sons of bitches.'"

"Where were you standing when he said that?"

"Right close to him."

Shoup continued questioning. "Did anything happen when he made that remark to you?"

"He made the remark and shot all at the same time," Anderson answered. "The first shot went right by my head, my ear, and I was reaching for him all the time. The next shot knocked me down. It hit me in the leg and rolled me behind the car. When I regained consciousness, I saw Evans lying in the middle of the street, and Tucker with his hands up, facing me."

"After these two shots that you have told the court about, did you hear any other shooting?"

"I did," Anderson affirmed for the court. "Just before I got turned around."

"Do you know how many shots were fired?"

"I can't answer that. More than one."

Shoup asked what happened next, and Anderson continued to explain the events of that night.

"Evans made the statement to Tucker, 'Get the gun and kill the son of a bitch.' I said, 'Don't move. Turn around,' to Tucker. He turned around. I hobbled over and kicked the gun away from Evans's hand, and picked it up and put it in my pocket."

"Where was Earl?" Shoup asked.

"I didn't know at that time. I thought, when I came to, that Earl had them covered because Tucker was standing there with his hands up. I couldn't see Earl, then I noticed him lying on the side of Columbus Street near Main. I walked over to where he was and shook him a bit, and he breathed one breath like, a deep breath. I knew I needed help so I walked Tucker over to Haller's filling station to use their telephone, but it was closed."

"Then what did you do?"

"Walked him back to the scene of the shooting. Finally, a fellow by the name of Rose—a colored man that lives in Xenia—came to my assistance."

Upon cross-examination by George Smith, Deputy Anderson said that although Doug James had warned "they might have a gun," he hadn't looked in the car for guns, but the deputies did search the boys when they got out of the Buick.

"When Tucker broke away from you, er, when Evans broke away from you, could you see where he got his gun?" Smith asked.

"No, sir," Anderson replied.

"Isn't it true, Joe, that when he came out with the gun that you lunged for it?"

"Just as soon as he went for the car I lunged for him," Anderson clarified.

"That's when he fired at you?"

"Yes."

The defense attorney then switched direction, asking about Tucker's role in the incident. Anderson responded that he wasn't questioning Tucker, but Smith continued anyway.

"He had his hands up, did he?" Smith asked about Tucker. "They remained up all the time, except you wouldn't know about the period you were unconscious, of course?"

"That's right."

"When you came to, his hands were still up?"

"That's right."

"Then he made no effort to comply with this request of Evans to, 'Get the gun and shoot the son of a bitch'?" Smith queried.

"No."

Prosecutor Shoup, seeming agitated, re-entered the questioning. "From and during the time that you say you were rolled over by this shot there on the street, Joe, do you know what Clarence Tucker was then doing?"

"No," Anderson responded.

"Do you know who shot Earl Confer?"

"No," Anderson testified and was excused.

Shoup next called Millard Schath, the Cincinnati detective, who told of how he heard about the crime en route to Dayton, and his trip to the Greene County Jail. He identified Tucker as the person he questioned and said

Tucker was asked where he got the gun, where he got the money for the purchase, and who paid for it. Schath said Tucker admitted to stealing and selling the whiskey and buying the revolver, as well as theft of the cars used on their trip to and from the Akron area.

Schath continued with his memory of what Tucker admitted about the gun. "He said, 'Well, we bought the gun. We had a stolen car and didn't intend to leave anyone take us into custody.' That was his explanation, " the detective testified.

George Smith immediately objected to this statement. "If that is true, it's an admission as to an essential element of the crime and is not admissible, the same as a confession, where that amounts to a confession of guilt. I ask that it be stricken."

"I don't exactly get your point," Judge Rankin said.

"He hasn't clarified his answer very much," said Smith, "as to whether there was an understanding that they were to shoot their way out. If taken as true, it's an admission of this man Tucker as to the essential elements of the crime in a first-degree murder case, the same as a confession of guilt. This, of course, is an essential element. The statute says you cannot plead guilty to a first-degree murder charge."

"Do I understand you to mean that a confession of guilt is not admissible in evidence?" Rankin asked.

"The statute says you can't plead guilty to a first-degree murder charge. How can an admission of the defendant alone..."

Judge Johnson interrupted. "You can plead guilty to a first-degree murder charge, and the Court hears the evidence. Objection overruled."

The Judge turned to Schath, in the witness stand. "Before Tucker made this statement to you, was there any promise or reward, or hope or favor held out to him?"

"There was not," Schath responded. "We advised him of his rights, that anything he said might be used against him or for him in court."

When Smith got his chance to cross-examine Schath, he continued to pursue the detective's claim for accuracy. "Mr. Schath, it is highly important that you should be quoting the witness correctly," Smith observed. "Do you know whether or not Tucker said, 'WE did not intend to be taken into custody,' or 'I did not intend to be taken into custody?'"

"It was plural, 'We,'" Schath replied.

"Where did he say that they made this agreement?"

"When they left Cincinnati in a stolen car that they wasn't going to be taken into custody by anyone."

Smith then asked if he had taken any notes on the interrogation, or whether Schath was relying on memory. "It was verbal," Schath replied.

"You are dependent on memory for its accuracy?"

"It was only a period of two months ago or a little better," the detective said.

"Isn't it true when they referred to the conspiracy to shoot that they referred to the robbery incident in Cincinnati?" Smith asked.

"There wasn't any robbery at Cincinnati."

"You just told me of one."

"That was a burglary," the officer corrected.

"Maybe I haven't got it right. They stole some whiskey from the hotel," the attorney adjusted his question.

"That is correct."

"Are you certain by what Tucker said that he wasn't referring to that time?"

"No. No. He was referring to both of them being in stolen cars—as he termed it 'hot' cars—and they didn't want to be caught."

"Did you make any threats when you went in there to talk to him?"

"I did not. There wasn't any threats, harsh words, or duress used against the man by anyone in my presence," Officer Schath assured the court.

"Didn't you make the statement, 'How would you like for us to take you back in there and work you over with blackjacks?'" the exasperated Smith asked.

"I did not, and no one else made that statement."

"You went in and explained his constitutional rights and told him that what he said could be used against him in a court of law, and it was completely voluntary?" Smith persisted in his questioning.

Officer Schath calmly replied, "That's correct."

Adolph Mezger, the other Cincinnati detective, followed on the stand. He gave his credentials and detailed his trip to Dayton. He told the court Tucker admitted the whiskey theft, car thefts, and the gun purchase.

"Then we asked him what he was going to do with the gun," Mezger said. "He said, well, nobody was going to apprehend us on this job, take us into custody."

"Did he make any statement about the shotgun that they had in their possession?" Shoup asked.

"Yes sir," Mezger politely responded. "I also asked him if he had done any shooting. He said he didn't do no shooting."

Smith returned to the questioning. " When you went into the cell there with Mr. Tucker, there was just you and Mr. Schath there?" he asked.

"No," Mezger replied. "The sheriff was there."

"Was there anyone there to represent Mr. Tucker?"

"No, sir."

"Did you advise him of his rights? To his constitutional rights?" Smith cross-examined.

"No, sir, my partner did that."

"What did you say to him?"

"Well, he—the first thing he asked him, 'Are you going to make a confession of the job you pulled?'" Mezger tried to explain.

Smith sought clarification here. "What job did he refer to?" he asked. In response, Mezger entered into a prolonged monologue on the stolen whiskey, the cars, and the purchase of the gun.

Smith sharpened his focus. "When you went in there, you went right into those matters you are now talking about, did you, Mr. Mezger?"

"Yes sir."

"And started questioning him about the robbery in Cincinnati, the automobile, and other matters in which he had been implicated?"

"Oh, yes."

Smith turned to the judges on the bench. "I move both of these statements be stricken for the reason that according to the testimony of this witness, the prisoner Tucker was not advised as to his constitutional rights," he said. "He was not told that the statements would be used against him in the trial. He was, of course, not represented by counsel, which is not so bad. They went right to the gist of things and did not ask him whether he was willing to make a voluntary statement. He just testified they did no such thing."

After a moment of thought, Judge Johnson responded to the motion, "I understand the other officer, Mr. Schath, did that."

"He said nobody did," Smith complained.

Shoup stepped in at this point. "He said Officer Schath, his partner, questioned the boy," Shoup said.

"He said they went right to the gist of the confession," Smith replied.

Now Judge Rankin entered the fray. He asked Smith to cite case law that would support the necessity of advising Tucker of his constitutional rights before interrogation, to which Smith could only reply that the confession had to be voluntary. His client, he said, had not received any counsel. "They didn't give him any chance at all," Smith concluded.

"'Voluntary' means not by coercion, or threats, or promises," Rankin said. "The question is, do you have any authority that it is necessary to advise the man of his constitutional rights before questioning him?"

"Not at this moment, I do not."

"I don't know of any," Judge Rankin sniffed.

Judge Johnson leaned forward toward the courtroom. "Overruled," he announced.

The prosecutor then called as its next witness, Col. Oznl H. Cornwell, the Superintendent of the Ohio State Bureau of Identification and Investigation, and a former Xenia Chief of Police. Shoup began the questioning.

"I would like for you to tell the court, to the best of your memory, just what was said by Mr. Tucker."

"I first told him we were conducting an investigation into the fatal shooting of Deputy Sheriff Earl Confer and the wounding of Officer Anderson," Cornwell said. "I asked him if he would make a statement as to his part in the shooting, and he said that he would. I cautioned him as to his rights under the Constitution of the United States, and that it was not required that he testify against himself, but he told me at the time he was willing to make a complete statement. We sent for Mrs. McFadden, the court stenographer."

"Before Mrs. McFadden came in, had he given you his version of this affair?" Shoup asked.

"He did."

"Then after Mrs. McFadden came, was a statement taken in question and answer form?"

"It was. I asked him to explain to us the chronological order of what led up to the shooting. He told us that he had known Evans since their days in school. We asked him why he purchased the revolver, and he first stated he didn't know, it was out of foolishness. In fact, the whole trip was out of foolishness. He claimed the ejection mechanism on the revolver was not working, and if he bought the gun and fixed the ejector, he could double his money by selling it in Cincinnati. I asked him why they had the shotgun in the car, and he answered, 'If someone was following us that the one not driving would fire the gun at the following car. Of course, it would not shoot very far, but it would be enough to mark the windshield and stop the people who were chasing us.'"

George Smith approached for cross-examination, probing for details regarding the interrogation that night. "You asked the further question, 'Well, did you have any conversation or understanding with Ernest that if anyone tried to stop you, you had a gun and would use it, and you had it for that purpose?' You asked that question?"

" I did," replied Cornwell.

"As a matter of fact, his answer was, 'We started them but we never finished them all the way, what we would do.' That was his answer?"

"Yes."

Smith asked Cornwell to clarify when the boys boasted they would 'shoot it out' with police, rather than be caught. Cornwell admitted the statement had been made in Cincinnati, in the context of taking the old shotgun.

Smith continued to expose the strategic details used in Tucker's questioning. "And then this question was asked: 'In other words, you discussed that angle with Evans and he discussed it with you, that wording, "shoot it out, if necessary," is that right?' And he said, 'He just made that agreement once, that's all.' Isn't that correct?"

"That's right," Cornwell said.

"All the way through here, you or some other officer or prosecutor gave statements of fact and asked him for yes or no answers?"

"That's right."

Smith rose up in summary: "So the statement of fact was given by your fellow officers, and not by Tucker himself. That's correct, isn't it?

"No."

"You said it was," Smith countered.

The witness was finally excused, and court was adjourned until 9:00 a.m. the following day. Before the crowd dispersed, however, Prosecutor Shoup stridently walked over to Joe Anderson, grabbed his arm, and pulled the husky, athletic black man through a door into a small room off the second-floor lobby in front of the courtroom entrance. It was time for what the veteran lawyers called "horse-shedding."

Shoup quietly closed the room's front door and briefly opened the back door a crack to see if anyone was in earshot, then pulled it shut. When he was assured the two were alone, he turned to Anderson. "Joe, you're killing us in there," Shoup said directly.

"What do you mean, Mr. Shoup?" replied the surprised Anderson.

"I mean, you're not putting Tucker into the scene," Shoup continued. "We won't get him convicted if people think he just stood there on the other side of the car."

"But that's what he did," Anderson responded.

"You know he was part of this shooting. Earl's dead. You're a member of the sheriff's department, aren't you? You want to stay a deputy, don't you?"

Years later, Anderson said in a deposition that the tone of this inquiry bothered him. He felt he had testified truthfully, but Shoup made it clear to him that his first testimony wasn't enough.

"Listen, Joe. We're going to put you back on the stand tomorrow," Shoup continued. "I'm going to ask you about how close Tucker was standing, and you need to say that he was right there with Earl. You got that?"

"Yessir."

"That's good. You just follow my lead."

Chapter 9

::

When the proceedings were reconvened early that Wednesday and court called to order, the state called Wayne Porter of Ravenna as the first witness. Porter, the clerk in the sporting goods store where Tucker bought the Harrington and Richardson revolver, identified Tucker as the man who bought the gun and displayed his sales slip showing that the gun was purchased by a "Sam Scott" of 15 W. Eighth Street, Newport, Kentucky. Next, the Greene County Engineer testified as to the width of the streets at the intersection of Main and Columbus, and the location of the vehicles at the intersection.

Then, Shoup recalled Deputy Joe Anderson to the stand, and a blackboard was rolled into the courtroom.

"Joe," he said, "in order to bring out just a little more clearly the positions of the automobiles and the persons who took part in this tragedy, I wonder if you, for the court, could make a drawing here on this blackboard of the street intersection and the automobiles."

Anderson began to draw lines and boxes with the chalk. At several points in the rendering, he asked Anderson to increase the size of the diagrams.

"Suppose we could get this street a little wider so when you get down to drawing the automobiles they will be a little larger. Now, does this represent Main Street?" Shoup asked, while writing "Main" and "Columbus."

"Now suppose you put the Buick car into position," Shoup said. "Just the way it was, as near as you can remember." Anderson drew a line to show the car's location.

"Make a rectangle out of it, instead of a line. Can't you make it a little larger?" Shoup asked and then continued. "Now suppose you put the Sheriff's car into position as it came to a stop."

Anderson drew a box as he was directed, but the diagram didn't suit the prosecutor.

"Joe, didn't you testify that the back of the Sheriff's car was part way on the side of the Buick?"

"Yes."

"You got too much difference between them if that is the case," Shoup corrected him.

Anderson adjusted his drawing, and Shoup began to ask him to indicate the locations of the four people involved in the incident.

"You all four were pretty close together?"

"Evans and I were standing here," Anderson answered and pointed.

"Put a cross there. Where was Earl?" Shoup continued. "Step back a little so Judge Brown can see."

"Confer and Tucker were standing right here," Anderson indicated, "looking at his driver's license."

"Those are the marks, right there?" Shoup continued to ask for specific locations, and then asked Anderson to draw each one and make corrections, to the extent that defense counsel George Smith complained. "He's trying to lead the witness," Smith said.

Judge Johnson agreed, but Shoup countered that he was merely trying to establish the location of the individuals involved. "I just wanted to clear that up," he said.

The final two witnesses for the state were Deputy Sheriff James R. Ramsey and Xenia Police Chief, Stanley Nickell. Both men said that Tucker admitted to a "pact" between the pair "to shoot it out with the police," but they both admitted under cross-examination that Shoup had made the statement, and Tucker said only that he and Evans had talked about a gun but once, in Cincinnati when the pair acquired the shotgun.

"Didn't this boy contend all during this interview that they had never had but one agreement, and that that agreement referred to the stealing of the liquor in Cincinnati?" Smith asked.

"The agreement was in Cincinnati, yes, about the guns," replied Nickell.

Smith's tactics apparently did not persuade Judge Rankin, however. "I understand your objection, which has been passed on, is on the grounds that this is what may be claimed to be an admission of guilt, and that that cannot be proven by admission. In other words, the authority you cited yesterday…"

"Do you want the citation?" Smith asked.

"No. The point that you raised, the grounds for your objection, just so we know, are the same as what you stated yesterday and gave a citation."

"I'm not so good at recalling what I said yesterday as some others that take the stand are of a month or two ago," responded Smith. "I don't know what I said in exact words, but it's my understanding from Ohio jurisprudence that where the admission goes to the essential elements of the crime, then it is not admissible, where it amounts to a confession of guilt, and that it must be proven by other evidence. That's the bare statement."

Shoup then announced that the state rested its case. George Smith rose. "If the court please," he said, "I thought at this time while you are in deliberations here, we would introduce a motion at the close of the State's testimony. The motion is that we now move that the purported confessions of Clarence Tucker to the effect that a conspiracy agreement between the two defendants to shoot their way out if apprehended be stricken from the record, for the reason that no other evidence except the purported confessions has been introduced indicating such a conspiracy.

"In support of that motion, I want to add that some cases have held that the evidence need only be in a case of conspiracy, and that is the rule laid down in several cases. I am introducing this as to the question of conspiracy alone. You had the acts, also, of what took place at the scene of the crime, which of course is in contradiction of the conspiracy. Other cases have held that the proof must be beyond a reasonable doubt. That is the law."

The tribunal of judges, led by my father, then entered into deliberation on the bench. After a few minutes of discussion, the presiding judge spoke: "Let the record show the motion of the defendants is overruled," he said.

The defense team called but one witness. Alice Evans had sat weeping through the first day's testimony. On the witness stand now, she noted that her son was only twenty years old, rather than twenty-one as the newspapers had reported. He held an honorable discharge from the Army Air Force, she added.

After lunch, Shoup and George Smith presented closing arguments. Then the three judges went into Judge Johnson's chambers to discuss their decision. Without recorded notes or comments, it's impossible to know exactly what was presented during the next thirty minutes, but it's fair to assume the judges acted characteristically. Judge Alton Brown, the quietest of the trio during the trial, would have relied on his long history as a lawyer and prosecuting attorney to evaluate the applicable law and the question of conspiracy. It was right there in the Ohio Criminal Code, No. 12402-1: "Whoever kills a...deputy sheriff...while in discharge of duties is guilty of murder in the First Degree and shall be punished by death." Judge Rankin likely concurred. The bottom line, he could have concluded, was that a police officer had been killed by the hand of one youth, using a gun owned by the other.

I recall that my father, Judge Johnson, had a reputation of a tendency toward leniency. He would have agreed that this clearly was a case of first-degree murder, but these were young men whose backgrounds had perhaps led them to act on a rash impulse. One of them was paying for his actions daily, as doctors continued to tend his wounds, and as he saw it, both of these young men would spend the rest of their lives behind bars in the state penitentiary. Wasn't that enough? Yet he recalled later that the original tally of the tribunal held, by a vote of two to one, that both boys were guilty of the murder of a police officer, and deserved the electric chair. Ultimately, however, it was my father, the presiding judge, who held the responsibility for their fate.

By mid-afternoon a verdict ended the trial. With the prosecution and defense teams and the gallery re-assembled, L. N. Shepherd, the Clerk of Court, read the tribunal's sparse statement: "We, the judges in this case, find the defendants, Ernest F. Evans and Clarence E. Tucker, each guilty, in the manner and form as they stand charged in the indictment, and do recommend mercy for each of said defendants."

When the verdict was announced, Evans relaxed a little and slumped in his wheelchair. Tucker, standing, showed no signs of emotion. Judge Johnson sought and received the approval of the defense to go directly to sentencing. The sentence was read twice, once for each youth. "The said Ernest F. Evans, having been found guilty of murder in the first-degree, with mercy recommended," Judge Johnson read. "It is therefore the sentence of the Court that the said Ernest F. Evans be imprisoned in the Penitentiary of this State and kept at hard labor for and during the balance of his natural life." He repeated the statement for Clarence E. Tucker.

Before dismissing the court, the judge cautioned the huge crowd against any demonstration. Then Tucker and Evans were taken back to the county jail. After three months, they were reunited in the same cell, together. *The Evening Gazette* report described them as joyous. Their lives had been spared.

Immediately following the trial, the three judges went into my father's chambers, removed their black robes, and exchanged handshakes. After saying goodbye and thanking the other judges for their service, Judge Johnson, now alone, lit a Lucky Strike, clamped it between his teeth and signed the document before him, a court order to the Sheriff of Greene County to remove the prisoners to the Ohio Penitentiary. After signing the order he sat back, relaxed, let out a sigh of relief, and enjoyed his cigarette.

Out in the courtroom, before the Smiths could leave, they were approached by Tucker's family, who first thanked them for their efforts. They questioned the Smiths about an appeal, but both members of the defense team assured the Tuckers that an appeal would not be a good idea. The sentence was as light and as fair as possible, they said, and an appeal could possibly revisit a death sentence. They told the Tuckers that in all likelihood, with good behavior Earl would be paroled within ten years. The Smiths reassured the Tuckers that everything possible had been done. Given the circumstances, the sentence of life in prison "was all we could expect," George Smith said.

For the prisoner Clarence Earl Tucker, ominous clouds of doubt had lifted. Three days after Easter, spring had arrived, and his own new life was about the begin. He knew that he had a future; the threat of having to sit in "Old Sparky," the electric chair, had vanished. But the events of the immediate past disturbed him greatly. He hadn't acted with malice toward anyone, yet here he was, preparing to spend the rest of his life in the Ohio Penitentiary. This sentence wasn't justice, and he wasn't going to accept it.

Chapter 10

::

"I *am sorry to hear about what those two boys got,*" I wrote in a letter to my parents in mid-May, while I was aboard the *USS Brush* in the South Pacific. At the time, I thought both boys were recent discharges from the military.

I imagine it was hard for Dad to do that, having a son so far away. I can understand why a person would change into a murderer in this environment. You are around all walks of life here, and the idea of being held back in everything you do and of being overruled constantly would change a person if he was in this outfit for a few years. You are constantly under scrutiny: while working, during leisure, and while on shore leave. You can never call your time your own. You're told what clothes to wear, what time you have to be in bed, when you must get up, and when to eat. If you do anything wrong, no matter how small the error, someone is yelling at you. They can insult you in every way, and you have to take it.

Yes, I can understand how some men would change after being held down like that.

I'm sorry I couldn't be home to go to the races with you.

~Sonny

After lunch on Thursday, April 25, Sheriff Spahr drove his official Greene County Sheriff's car to the front of the jail. Deputies Henry E. Barnett and the sheriff's cousin, Deputy Homer Spahr, led the two handcuffed prisoners to the waiting automobile. Like all the Spahrs, Walton and Homer were robust men with barrel chests. The pair filled the front seat and blocked the view of the backseat occupants. Deputy Barnett sat in the back seat between Tucker and Evans, who was in a degree of discomfort. His wound was draining badly. He tried to rest and said little.

Within two minutes, the car passed the corner of Market Street and Columbus Avenue, where just three months ago Tucker had run a red light, drawing the attention of Deputies Anderson and Confer. After another fifteen minutes on twisting, hilly Route 42 the car passed the Rainbow Inn. Somehow, possibly with daylight, the restaurant seemed larger. Perhaps, the lights at night had illuminated the café differently. Twenty minutes later, the cruiser passed through London, which Evans and Tucker had used for playful target practice.

The day was warm, with a temperature in the upper 60s. There was a chance of rain. They were passing through prime farm land with black, rich soil. Some of the farmers were plowing or pulling a disc to prepare the fields for beans. A few planted corn.

"Take a good look around you, boys, it will be a long time before you get a chance to see this again," one of the officers remarked. Sheriff Spahr rolled down the window to let in a little fresh air. Within another hour, the Greene

County car arrived at the Ohio Penitentiary, on Spring Street near downtown Columbus, to discharge its cargo.

The two shackled boys were led first to an office where a clerk, pen in hand, opened a great book, the Register of Prisoners, and began leafing through its thick pages until he reached blank lines on page 370. Evans stepped forward, and an officer at his back announced his name. "F-I-N-L-E-Y," Evans corrected the scribe, who added the further necessary information: "Age 20, white. Rec'd Ohio Pen. April 25, 1946. Murder 1st deg. (mercy)." With that, Ernie Evans became prisoner number 83750.

Tucker followed: "Age 20, W. Rec'd Apr. 25, 1946. Term: LIFE," scribbled at at angle adjacent to "Min.-Max." He became prisoner number 83751.

After a great deal of paperwork, prisoners 83750 and 83751 were strip-searched, deloused, and allowed to shower. They were weighed, measured, and issued their striped gray prison uniforms. Once dressed, the two were fingerprinted, photographed, and handed the "Inmate Manual: Handbook of Information & Regulation Governing Men Committed to the Ohio State Penitentiary." In its pages they were warned "not to tear, write in, or mar this book. You will be required to turn in this book at your final 'shakedown.'" Then, they were separated. Evans was taken to the prison hospital, as he was still sick and in pain. Tucker was led to his cell, and when the door clanged shut behind him, the new inmate inspected his surroundings through its iron bars, counting three tiers of cells, holding what appeared to be almost endless rows of caged men. This was to be his world inside the walls.

Outside, back in Xenia, full front pages of *The Evening Gazette* bid goodbye to Tucker and Evans. Having held the presses on Wednesday until the verdict was announced, the paper blared the decision with a huge headline spanning page one, followed by a breathless bulletin announcing the decision of the three-judge panel in bold type. A day later came a startling announcement, once again in bold headlines:

CONVICTED KILLERS REMOVED TO PRISON; CARVED GUN FOUND

Believe Tucker May Have Planned Break With Imitation Weapon; Defense Not To Appeal Verdict By Judges

The news seemed to confirm what everyone had known: the two boys were thugs who apparently had planned to bust out in a blaze of glory. At least that's what Prosecutor Shoup suggested in the dramatic front-page article that served as a denouement to his court victory. "The imitation gun," Shoup disclosed, "probably made by the accused slayer with the thought of using it as an 'out' if given the death penalty, was to have been entered as evidence when the two defendants took the stand," *The Gazette* reported.

According to Shoup, Tucker had used shaving razor blades to carve the "realistic replica of a .38 caliber revolver," using wood from his cell bench and soap, which was then blackened with paint from model airplane kits. Sheriff Spahr, Chief Deputy Henry Barnett, and Deputy C. P. Mahan had discovered the ruse, including a map of the jail, some three weeks prior to the trial. "Tucker had guns on his mind even while facing trial for his life," Shoup told *The Gazette*. He added that the trio of officers had replaced the model and increased their surveillance of Tucker.

According to Shoup, he kept Tucker's alleged handiwork secret until after the trial. Years later, Tucker's attorney in subsequent court action expressed surprise that his client would have, or could have, produced a bogus weapon. "I wouldn't believe that on a stack of Bibles," said Irving Harris. "Clarence was a quiet guy. Clarence could not have pulled the trigger on a gun. That gun was a plant."

Circumstantial evidence would seem to support the attorney's claim. The simple tools given to Tucker to build his model airplanes would have been insufficient to carve off a piece of the one-inch stock of his bench. In addition, Shoup said that Tucker had pried one of the bench boards loose to hide the gun, but the prisoner had no tools sturdy enough to pull a floor board. And suspiciously, the "gun" was never displayed to the public.

On the other hand, Tucker in the Xenia jail faced a capital murder conviction with hometown counsel whose tactics suggested surrender. It's clear he felt that justice wasn't being served, and one way or another, he would earn the freedom he was due. That was obvious from his activities almost immediately following the trial.

Within months of his incarceration, Tucker began to prepare documents seeking a new trial. The Tucker family had approached the Smiths immediately after the trial verdict, asking the defense counsel to investigate an appeal, but the Smiths said that reopening the case would place Clarence in renewed jeopardy. Besides, they said, with good behavior, Clarence would be freed in about ten years. Their reluctance must have been disappointing for Tucker, who had assumed his court-appointed attorneys would continue working on his behalf. Prison inmate rolls show that his family members visited only rarely, so Tucker must have realized he was once again on his own. Within the prison walls, probably advised by fellow inmates or library documents, he prepared his own petition for a new trial.

The request went nowhere. All inmate correspondence had to be funneled through prison officials via a "kite," an approved form, and when Tucker attempted to mail his document, it was intercepted and returned with a note. Tucker could proceed with court action only through legal counsel, the warden said. The Smiths would not help, and his family couldn't. He was stranded.

The lives of Tucker and Evans thus melted into the routine of the prison. "Consider the ways necessary to change your daily habits . . . so that you may become better adjusted to the new situation in which you find yourself," the prison manual suggested. "Here, you are under the constant supervision of others. Learn to conform and comply with the rules of this small society, and you will . . . help yourself become adjusted." These directives, designed in the nineteenth century when the rock edifice was built, required prisoners to rise at 6:45 a.m. for reveille and to present themselves for the daily morning "count" at 7:00 a.m. Then, in silence, they marched "in a military manner," in columns of threes at the command "Forward, march!" to dining halls for breakfast at 7:10 a.m. Shop work or school began at 7:30 a.m., lunch at 11:00 a.m., and supper at 4:00 p.m., followed by the evening "institutional count" at 4:50 p.m. Lights were extinguished at 9:45 p.m., after which talking was strictly prohibited.

Tucker and Evans were just two of the more than 5,000 prisoners stuffed into a facility experiencing exploding population growth. Inmates coexisted in cells with either two or three roommates, or as time progressed, in dormitories. They ate miserable food. "They would give us butter beans with a piece of fat sowbelly in there with hair on it, big hairs up to an inch long," recalled one man who was imprisoned during the 1940s. In 1952, prisoners rioted in response to the bad food.

The rebellion came despite a reform campaign instituted by a new warden, Ralph Alvis, in the late 1940s. Under the new regime, prisoners enjoyed expanded recreation programs, and inmates were treated with more dignity. They staged a popular annual Christmas show, organized musical entertainment, and filled the roster of an exceptional amateur softball team, the "Hurricanes."

Tucker apparently adjusted well to prison life. His record indicates that, due to his excellent record of behavior, in August 1955, he earned a transfer out of the walls to work as head of commissary operations at the minimum-security London Prison Farm. Ten years earlier, Tucker and Evans had passed a few miles south of the farm, distributing mayhem en route to Xenia. A few months later, they passed again, going in the other direction and accompanied by sheriff's deputies delivering them to the Penitentiary. Now, Tucker supervised the kitchen for the 300 other inmate-employees who tended cultivated rows and enjoyed the relative freedom of dormitory living.

Unfortunately, his stay at the London Prison Farm was brief. On May 18, 1956, Tucker was rushed back to the Ohio Penitentiary Hospital for an unidentified medical emergency. He did not return to the farm. During the next decade, however, he retained his honor inmate status. One assignment, at the penitentiary's Marietta honor camp, temporarily got him outside the prison walls again. He also earned real money—two cents an hour—making leather products that the prison sold.

Another assignment in the prison library turned Tucker into a bookworm. "I never enjoyed playing cards, so I didn't waste time playing them," he once told a reporter who asked about his time behind bars. Instead, after work in the library, he read its books. Tested by a prison psychiatrist, Tucker was rated with the educational equivalent two years of college.

And he continued to use his hands. Tucker took up chess, and using plywood as a base, he created a fine chessboard inlaid with different kinds of wood. "They say chess is a way of life," he explained to the reporter.

His friend Ernie Evans also became an honor inmate, but he took a different path. Unlike Tucker, Evans went directly to the prison hospital after his intake registration at the penitentiary. Although Greene County jail physician R. L. Haines had tended to his bullet wound and subsequent infection, the wound never completely healed while Evans was incarcerated in the county facilities after the 1946 shooting. Upon Evans's departure for Columbus, Dr. Haines explained to reporters that doctors had removed about eight inches of the boy's intestines during the prisoner's emergency treatment at Miami Valley Hospital the morning of the shooting, and the patient had developed "terrific peritonitis."

Evans would have to undergo further surgery in prison, which he might not survive. "He has a long way to go for recovery," Dr. Haines, the jail physician, said, adding that even if Evans recovered, "he will never be normal."

Records indicate that after his initial treatment, Evans recovered enough without surgery to be in the general prison population for about two years. He enjoyed visits about once a month from loyal family members, including his mother Alice, his father Grant, brother James, and sisters Anita and Edna Mae, who had divorced John Boggs in Ravenna and was living with her second husband, Robert Muir, and daughter in Cincinnati. But in the fall of 1948, Evans was readmitted to the prison hospital in worsening condition.

Family members drove up from Cincinnati more frequently, as much as once a week during the Christmas season that year. Then, with the new year, Ernie's condition deteriorated, and prison doctors were unable to reverse his decline. As he weakened, he began to think more seriously about his life, the events that had put him into his situation, and the questionable legal decision that had incarcerated his friend, Clarence Earl Tucker.

It's unclear how much Tucker and Evans were able to communicate during their imprisonment. Although they weren't roommates, the pair were not physically separated, and in the more relaxed atmosphere of the reformed prison environment, they could have conversed with one another relatively freely. Evans obviously knew that Tucker had tried to begin new legal proceedings. He wanted to help. He could explain the truth of his actions almost exactly three years earlier, that morning in Xenia.

Evans acquired the services of a notary public to support the veracity of his thoughts, and penned the following statement:

> *To Whom It May Concern:*
>
> *Concerning the charge of First Degree Murder for which I am under sentence at the Ohio Penitentiary, I, Ernest Evans, knowing that I have but a very short time to live, voluntarily and of my own free will, wish to make the following statement:*
>
> *At no time prior to the appearance of the officers at the scene of the shooting, which took place in connection with the crime for which I am*

under sentence, was there any plan in any shape or form to resist any arrest or any attempted arrest. It was after both my companion and myself had been placed under arrest that I obtained permission to return to the car to turn the headlights out, that I noticed the revolver lying on the seat of the car and without stopping to consider the consequences of my act, either to myself or my companion, I reached for the revolver and demanded the officers raise their hands. After Officer Anderson attempted to take the revolver away from me, panic seized me and I remember nothing clearly after that. My actions were entirely the result of a sudden and unaccountable impulse on my part, which I can ascribe only to a sudden seizure of panic.

Ernest Evans
No. 83750
Ohio Penitentiary

Signed and sworn to by Ernest Evans
in my presence this 22nd day of
January, 1949, at Columbus, Ohio.
E.L. Maxwell
Notary Public, Franklin Co.
State of Ohio.

It was the clearest statement yet of what had happened that cold morning. Without the opportunity to take the witness stand to speak for themselves, Tucker and Evans had let their counsel, the prosecutor, and the judges frame the motivations of the young men when they were put under arrest. Whereas Shoup had argued, in the absence of any alternative view, that the defendants were two hoodlums acting in a premeditated agreement to shoot it out with police, in his writing Evans testified clearly that he had pulled the trigger purely, and characteristically, in a spontaneous impulse.

Despite the deathbed nature of Evans's penitent statement, he did survive. In February 1949, doctors performed radical and experimental surgery that brought the prisoner back from the brink. Evans was revived, and so was Tucker's legal effort.

Chapter 11

::

Evans's letter gave Earl Tucker ammunition for a renewed legal battle. He had quit his court-appointed attorneys shortly after he was deposited in the penitentiary, because the Smiths had given his family bad advice. At his sentencing, they had declined to file an appeal, believing they had done the best job possible and suggesting that Clarence could be free in a decade. In truth, the Ohio Criminal Code required that in cases involving the death of a police officer, the guilty party would serve a minimum of twenty years in prison.

The working-class Tucker family couldn't afford to hire expensive legal counsel to examine Clarence's situation. In fact, Grandfather Claude was able to provide living accommodations for himself, his wife Ella, and Popeye and Mary only because the family did maintenance work in their Bishop Street apartment building for the landlord, Albert Harris. Harris, a real estate developer, also employed Popeye as a janitor at the nearby Telford Apartments, and it was there that he mentioned his legal problems to his employer. Harris, it turned out, had a son, Irving, just out of the University of Cincinnati Law School, who might be interested in the case.

In 1952, Irving Harris was a Navy veteran with a new position in the Cincinnati law firm, Cors, Shearer, Hair & Hartsock. With a specialty in commercial law, he had worked on several banking and bankruptcy cases involving millions of dollars, but he had done only a few criminal cases, which in the scale of his firm were "miniscule," by his own admission. But he saw Tucker's situation as a new challenge.

Attorney Irving Harris in a 1966 photo (Photo courtesy of Irving Harris)

"Defending Clarence was not my regular kind of practice, " Harris recalled. "I did it for his father, Popeye. I didn't expect any kind of pay, because they didn't have any money. My thesis was that I was a trial lawyer, and a good trial lawyer can try anything."

"I thought it was an interesting case," Harris added. "They said he's been up in jail, and he needs help. He was guilty of theft. He was guilty of bad company. But he just stood there. He was wallpaper."

"All he wanted was out. Popeye wanted him out," Harris continued. "They were just looking for vindication."

"I always felt that it was challenging. People would always threaten me—you can't do this, you can't do that. My response was, 'We're gonna try this case.' There was one lawyer in our firm who said, 'Irving, don't do that case. What if they retry and send him to the electric chair?' I said we'll cross that bridge when we get to it."

Harris found the first obstacle to confront was his own inexperience in criminal law. Working with a good researcher and competent trial lawyer, Robert O. Edington,

Harris sought from the Greene County Common Pleas court a writ of habeas corpus, a request to take Tucker out of prison for a hearing to seek a new trial. In Tucker's name, Harris also submitted a formal request that Greene County supply a transcript of the original trial testimony at no cost, because as an Ohio State Penitentiary inmate, Tucker was without funds.

It had been seven years since the trial, but the Presiding Judge continued to be my father, Judge Frank Johnson. He didn't look with favor on their request and took the young attorneys to task for their effort. In a letter dated June 30, 1953, the Judge pointed out that "any application for a writ of habeas corpus would have to be filed in the county in which the prisoner is confined. Therefore, this Court would have no jurisdiction to pass on any of the matters set forth in your motion."

The legal lesson continued: "For your information be advised that at the hearing of this case originally Mr. Tucker was represented by counsel, to wit: former Judge of the Common Pleas Court of Greene County, George H. Smith, and former Judge of the Municipal Court of Xenia, E. D. Smith, and all of his rights were fully protected." The Judge assured Harris that Tucker had waived a jury trial in favor of the tribunal, and he reminded Harris that the death penalty could have been imposed but for the leniency of one judge.

"How at this time any application for habeas corpus could be filed with any success would be beyond me," the Judge concluded.

Tucker must have been sorely disappointed at the scolding given to the attorneys on his behalf. At least with eager legal help, he could live a more hopeful life inside the prison walls. He couldn't know that outside the walls society was evolving dramatically, in ways that would favor his struggle.

Within the penitentiary, inmates were allowed to listen to the radio only during "music hours," between 2:00 and 4:00 p.m., and for an additional hour at 7:00 p.m. In the outside world, the media had became pervasive and ubiquitous, as Samuel Holmes Sheppard learned to his dismay. Early in July 1954, Sheppard, a popular osteopathic physician in Bay Village, a suburb of Cleveland, told police he had fallen asleep watching television and had awakened to a noise in his lakefront home. He claimed he struggled with someone in the dark, found his wife murdered, and chased a tall man with dark bushy hair across his lawn. Some two hours later a friend, called by Sheppard, arrived to find a bloody crime scene. Next, came police and the Cuyahoga County coroner, Dr. Samuel Gerber, who vividly described the murder victim's wounds for reporters.

The story quickly became front-page news. A few days after the crime, the county coroner and "Dr. Sam," as Sheppard was known in the community, accompanied police for a tour of the scene, where they confronted a horde of sightseers, photographers, and reporters who had been given permission to cover the event. Soon, newspaper editorials demanded an arrest in the case, while accompanying news stories linked Sheppard romantically with a woman other than his deceased wife. Media pressure intensified, and community emotions ran high until the *Cleveland Press* published an eight-column editorial that demanded immediate action, after which Sheppard was arrested, tried, and ultimately convicted of second-degree murder.

Sheppard vigorously claimed innocence. Repeated efforts to gain an appeal were filed without success, until in 1961, his family hired the aggressive young attorney F. Lee Bailey. In April 1963, Bailey filed a writ of habeas corpus in federal court, claiming that the excessive media coverage in the case, with the trial judge's failure to grant a change of venue, had doomed Dr. Sam. A federal judge in Dayton, Ohio, agreed. "If there ever was a trial by newspaper, this is a perfect example," said Judge Carl Weinman in his decision. Further legal challenges took the Sheppard case to the U.S. Supreme Court, which in 1966 ruled that "The massive, pervasive and prejudicial publicity attending the petitioner's prosecution prevented him from receiving a fair trial."

Aggressive police questioning also came under scrutiny during the decades of Tucker's incarceration. About the time Tucker returned to the Ohio Penitentiary from his brief stay at the London Farm, a teenager in the southwestern state of Arizona named Ernesto Arturo Miranda began a career of petty crime that paralleled Tucker's early years. Indeed, at one point Miranda was serving time at the federal prison in Chillicothe, Ohio, even while Tucker was about seventy miles north, in the Ohio Penitentiary.

Miranda eventually moved to Phoenix, Arizona, where in 1963, he was arrested for kidnapping and rape. He confessed after two hours of police interrogation, during which police neglected to inform Miranda of his right to remain silent and to have representation. He was convicted at trial, but immediately sought an appeal that eventually was joined by the American Civil Liberties Union, which argued before the United States Supreme Court that his Sixth Amendment rights had been violated.

The High Court agreed to hear the case in order to clarify the law following its controversial 5-4 ruling in Escobedo v. Illinois, in which the defendant had been denied the opportunity to meet with counsel. By the same 5-4 majority, the Supreme Court overturned Miranda's conviction in Miranda v. State of Arizona. "If the individual indicates in any manner, at any time prior to or during questioning, that he wishes to remain silent, the interrogation must cease. . . . If the individual states that he wants an attorney, the interrogation must cease until an attorney is present. At that time, the individual must have an opportunity to confer with the attorney and to have him present during any subsequent questioning," Chief Justice Earl Warren wrote in his majority opinion.

For Tucker's attorney Irving Harris, the high-profile decisions in Sheppard, Escobedo, and Miranda put in place the final pillars of precedent for Tucker's effort to win a new trial. The main support for Tucker, however, was as much the result of Ohio state politics as it was evolution of legal precedent. Following the initial rejection by

Judge Johnson, Harris had made repeated attempts to seek clemency through the Ohio Parole Board, but each effort was denied on grounds that the legal issues presented to the Board should have been dealt with in a court of law. By tradition, the Board would not recommend a commutation of the life sentence given to anyone convicted in the death of a police officer. That tradition continued through the 1950s, even in the administration of the relatively liberal Governor Michael V. DiSalle, who opposed capital punishment, and who, before leaving the governor's office in 1962, issued commutations for seven convicted murderers. "The right of clemency is a constitutional responsibility, which is a part of our system of justice," DiSalle said.

DiSalle's preference for mercy apparently included neither Tucker nor Evans, despite repeated applications by both inmates for review of their cases between 1953 and 1966. It took a change of administrations, strangely to a conservative governor who viewed social activism as anathema.

James Allen Rhodes took office in 1962 after handily defeating DiSalle on a platform of "jobs and progress." Rhodes, a crafty career politician without a college degree, had fashioned a proletarian persona that matched his southern Ohio dialect. He tirelessly promoted the State of Ohio and low taxes for production of its products, dished out home-spun wisdom, and deftly passed weighty matters of government to his able lieutenants, notably Chief of Staff John McElroy.

McElroy, described as "a bookish, articulate lawyer," absorbed the controversies surrounding murder convictions in Ohio to the extent that no one knew Rhodes's view of capital punishment. McElroy's quiet, careful attention to the issues, cases, and personalities in fact promoted commutations of prisoners' sentences and stifled executions in Ohio during Rhodes's first eight years in office.

McElroy kept files on both Tucker and Evans, no doubt prompted by their repeated applications for parole and their spotless records of good behavior. He spoke with Irving Harris and corresponded with Tucker, who by 1966 had served a full twenty years in the penitentiary. Tucker had eagerly awaited a Parole Board commutation hearing that spring, and when the Board declined to recommend a commutation, McElroy recognized Tucker's disappointment in a letter to the inmate dated June 3 of that year. The governor's representative explained the Board's reluctance due to its traditional position on mercy for cop killers, and he added that Rhodes "would not grant a commutation in the absence of a recommendation from the Parole Board." Tucker's next opportunity to see a commutation would be in five years, McElroy said.

McElroy further recommended that Tucker and Harris revisit an alternative strategy that they had discarded in favor of the commutation hearing. As early as 1955, the American legal community had formulated a uniform policy to deal with cases in which individuals remained imprisoned despite subsequent changes in the law or criminal procedures. Though such retroactive analysis obviously was controversial, the impetus toward such reviews, called post-conviction remedies, had by the early 1960s spread to many states, including Ohio. In July of 1965, the Ohio Legislature, influenced by an Illinois law, enacted Section 2953.21 of the Ohio Revised Code, a "Petition to vacate or set aside sentence" stating:

> *A prisoner in custody under sentence and claiming a right to be released on the ground that there was such a denial ... of his rights as to render the judgment void or voidable under the Ohio Constitution or the Constitution of the United States, may file a verified petition at any time in the court which imposed the sentence....*
>
> *...The court shall...grant a prompt hearing thereon, determine the issues, and make findings of fact and conclusions of law....*
>
> *If the court finds that there was such a denial or infringement of the rights of the prisoner, ...it shall vacate and set aside the judgment....*

"It is for you and your attorney to decide," McElroy suggested, "but it seems to me that there are good reasons to proceed under the post-conviction remedy statute."

Tucker and Harris were persuaded. For years, Harris and his colleague Edington had been stymied by Ohio law that restricted the use of habeas corpus for appeal of murder cases. Without a right to speak in court, any attempt to win a new trial would be useless. "In those days, the criminal laws were very strict," Harris recalled. "Then along came this brand new law." He was further prodded by McElroy's observation that Deputy Joseph Anderson, the black jailer wounded in the 1946 shooting and the only trial witness still alive, supported Tucker's commutation (but opposed one for Evans). Harris and Edington hustled to find the retired officer and were rewarded with surprising documentation.

"The black officer who wasn't killed in the shooting was a big break for us. He was a good guy," Harris said. "We got a very detailed statement—a signed statement. It was beneficial to us. It was very accurate."

"Anderson was quite open when we got his statement," Harris added. "He was told he was putting Tucker too far from the action."

Being coerced into revised testimony had irritated Anderson for years. "He said Clarence wasn't about to shoot anybody," said Harris, who used the name by which Tucker was known in court. "He said Clarence had been railroaded, and he was willing to testify to that."

Through the summer and fall of 1966, Harris and Edington prepared their case. In December, they sent a copy of their argument to Tucker in prison, asking for his signature. He approved by signing a notarized response on December 14, saying the facts and allegations stated in the document were a truthful account. On December 20, Harris and Edington filed a petition and a 35-page supporting brief to the Common Pleas Court of Greene County to "vacate or set aside the sentence" of Petitioner Clarence

E. Tucker, and a motion for a hearing in which Tucker, Anderson, and other witnesses could testify, and evidence could be presented. A score of years earlier, Prosecutor Shoup had used language in the indictment that mimicked the Ohio Criminal Code to show that the crime of which Tucker and Evans were accused fit the letter of the law. In their bid for a new hearing, Tucker's attorneys wrote a script that followed the letter of the post-conviction remedy law, suggesting that Tucker had been found guilty unjustly in April 1946, sentenced, and incarcerated since then in the Ohio Penitentiary. "There was a denial and infringement of his rights so as to render the judgment of the three-judge panel void or voidable under the Ohio Constitution, the Constitution of the United States, and the Statutes of Ohio in the following respects," stated the petition. They went on to cite the Miranda and Escobedo cases to illustrate the impropriety of Tucker's interrogations, the Sheppard Supreme Court decision to suggest that "inflammatory and prejudicial newspaper articles and editorials" should have prompted a change of venue, and gave a host of examples from the original transcript to show the ineffectiveness of Tucker's counsel during the original trial.

"Your petitioner, who has served twenty years in the Ohio Penitentiary, further submits that justice will be served only when his present sentence is vacated and a new trial granted," the brief concluded.

Chapter 12

::

Toward the end of the war, my father observed that my older sister, Nancy, could type briskly and write shorthand uncommonly well. Seeing this talent, he set her up for a job with Xenia attorney Dan M. Aultman, a close family friend who raised show chickens on a farm south of town. Of medium height, a bit paunchy and disheveled, Aultman, with his distracted demeanor and cluttered office, gave the impression of inattention. During the seven years Nancy served as his secretary, she would tell stories of taking dictation as Aultman paced the floor like a caged rooster. Yet Aultman became something of a protege to my father, following in the Judge's footsteps to be appointed (by my father) as Xenia's municipal court judge, a position he held from 1935 to 1939, and then to be elected as successor to my father as judge of the Common Pleas Court of Greene County, starting in 1955. Aultman was a popular judge, ultimately elected four times to six-year terms on the bench.

Judge Dan Aultman on the bench (Photo courtesy of Greene County Public Library Greene Room--Local History and Genealogy, Xenia, Ohio)

So it happened that in the last days of 1966, Dan Aultman, as judge of the Greene County Common Pleas Court, found himself studying a petition. It would grant a new trial for a man his mentor, Judge Johnson, had pronounced guilty of first-degree murder twenty years before.

Irving Harris stood before Judge Aultman on January 6, 1967, in Greene County Common Pleas Court, referring to the document he had filed two weeks earlier. His client, Clarence Earl Tucker, deserved the right to appear in the court to testify on his own behalf, he said. Judge Aultman took a little more than a week to review the brief and consider the attorney's request, and on January 17, he announced, "The court finds that said application is well taken and should be sustained."

"Therefore," Judge Aultman wrote, "it is hereby ordered that the Sheriff of Greene County, Ohio, produce the body of Clarence E. Tucker before this court on February 9, 1967."

In the intervening weeks, tragedy interrupted the hopeful renewal of Case No. 8101, State of Ohio, Plaintiff, v. Clarence E. Tucker, et al., Defendants. On January 10, 1967, Joseph Anderson, the wounded police officer who had agreed to support Tucker's effort for freedom, died at the age of 63 at his home in Yellow Springs. He had been in California for the Rose Bowl Game in Pasadena, suffered a heart attack following the game, and lingered in ill health for several days after being brought back to Ohio. With his death, the last witness to testify in the original trial was lost.

: :

Clarence Earl Tucker sniffed freezing cold air when he returned to Xenia on Thursday, February 9, 1967, in the back seat of a Greene County Sheriff's cruiser. It had been twenty-one years since he was a guest of the county, and so much had changed in the world that it seemed he was visiting a different planet.

When Tucker first was driven behind the big limestone walls of the Ohio Penitentiary, men worked in factories, and women took care of children in the home. Families gathered around big console-style radios in the living room for audio entertainment, perhaps by the big bands, or perhaps by soap operas or serials featuring famous Hollywood movie stars. Fast steam locomotives could carry passengers across the country in a couple of days, and the Army Air Force was just beginning to utilize planes powered by jet engines. American military power, with emphasis added by the fearsome atomic bomb, dominated the world.

In 1967, Tucker was transported out of prison into a troubled society. Women who had sampled empowering employment during World War II now demanded economic and sexual freedom, while men who had taken advantage of the GI Bill moved away from industrial assembly lines to middle-class suburban homesteads. People of color were in the middle of a struggle to throw off the old Jim Crow ways that excluded and demeaned, while at the same time music born in black ghettos and sharecroppers' plots had morphed into rock n' roll and its derivatives, and television was becoming the focus of popular culture. Transcontinental air travel in a few hours quickened American society, which was being cleaved by military involvement in Southeast Asia. In Ohio, politicians were even numbering the days of the old Ohio Penitentiary, as its facilities crumbled.

In Xenia, Russell Bradley, a stocky Kentuckian who sported a flat-topped crew cut, now held the title of Sheriff. Bradley enjoyed the company of a large staff of deputies, of whom it was said all had Kentucky birth certificates. Tucker found them much more accommodating for his visit in the Greene County Jail this time. "They kind of liked him," recalls Harris. "They brought him burgers and stuff."

Earl Tucker in prison garb at the start of his 1967 hearing (Photo courtesy of Greene County Public Library Greene Room--Local History and Genealogy, Xenia, Ohio)

Judge Aultman had originally scheduled Tucker's hearing for Thursday, but Harris remembers that he was silenced by a bout of laryngitis, so Tucker's court appearance was postponed a day. Perhaps that was why Tucker's hearing commenced in an inauspicious fashion: unlike his first appearance in court years before, when he wore a suit and tie, Tucker arrived at the courthouse on this cold, windy day escorted by a lone Sheriff's deputy and dressed in denim prison garb. His father had brought decent civilian clothes, but when the hearing was delayed, they were not delivered to Tucker until later in the day.

Irving Harris addressed that issue immediately upon opening his case, apologizing to the court for Tucker's appearance. Then, in a perhaps inadvertent reference to original testimony in the case, he declined an opening statement in order "to get into the gist of the matter" by immediately calling Tucker to the witness stand. The defendant, a boy at the time of the crime and now a middle-aged man, would at last get a chance to tell his story in court.

Led by Harris's questions, Tucker identified himself as a 41-year-old resident of the Ohio State Penitentiary who had been confined for "twenty years and nine months and some days." He described driving on State Route 42 to Xenia that dark morning in January 1946, passing through a yellow caution light at an intersection, hearing a siren, and seeing red lights blinking on a sheriff's car in his rear-view mirror. Ernest Evans was with him in the car, and there was a gun. "It was in the glove compartment," Tucker said. "So far as I know, it was unloaded. When I placed it there, it was unloaded."

In a dialogue of brief questioning and response, Tucker narrated the encounter on the street. He and Evans got out of the Buick, answered questions, and heard Anderson and Confer agree to place them under arrest.

"Evans requested permission to get in the car to turn out the lights," Tucker said. "He got in the car, turned out the lights, and came out with the revolver."

"And what did, what happened next? What occurred?" Harris asked.

"Officer Anderson lunged at him—the shot was fired," Tucker responded. "Anderson fell down and just at the same instant Confer gave me a shove out of the way, away from him. By the time I got turned around, there was a series of shots. Evans was here, Confer next to the curb, and Anderson lying near the rear wheel."

"Everybody on the ground?" Harris asked.

"Everybody on the ground."

Tucker added that for the next half minute, he was the only conscious man at the scene. He said he thought Evans was dead, and Confer wasn't moving. Then Anderson regained consciousness, got to his feet, and kicked the gun away from Evans, who by now "was shouting for me to get the gun and shoot the S.O.B.," Tucker said.

Harris now tried to rebuild the recently deceased Deputy Anderson's observations. "Were you present at the trial at which Officer Anderson testified?" Harris asked.

"Yes."

"Could you recall his being asked whether you had your hands up?"

"Yes."

"And do you recall his answer being you did?"

"Yes."

"And do you recall his being asked if you offered any resistance to any police officer?"

"Yes."

"And do you recall what his answer was?"

At this point, Greene County's representative in the case, Assistant Prosecuting Attorney John Neatherton, had heard enough. "I object," he said. "Ask him, rather than lead him." Judge Aultman agreed.

"I have to reiterate the statements," Harris replied. "It's the only possible way to ask the questions." Also, he might have added, the only way to bring back the valuable testimony of his lost witness. He turned to Tucker on the witness stand. "Do you recall his answer?"

"His answer was no. There was no resistance," Tucker said.

Tucker continued to describe the circumstances of his arrest and initial confinement. He had been awake for about twenty hours, and he was totally confused, he said. His first interrogations, with Cincinnati Detectives Mezger and Schath, accompanied by a county deputy "and two newspaper men," seemed to leave the greatest impression in his memory. Millard Schath, he recalled, asked most of the questions.

"Did he make any verbal threats to you?" the attorney asked.

"He informed me firmly how I would be treated if this had happened in Cincinnati. Possibly beaten to death by them," Tucker said. To further questions, Tucker testified that they did not advise him of a right to consult with an attorney or to remain silent.

"And did they advise you of what you were suspected of, or leave the implication?" Harris asked.

"They left it to implication."

Neatherton interrupted at this point. "I would like to have this man testify rather than you ask him continuously," he said. "I am going to object to the way the questions are being asked. I want to hear the story same as anybody else, but I would like to hear it from him."

Judge Aultman decided at this point it was time for a little mediation. He called Harris, a short, stocky man, and Neatherton, a tall, slender attorney, to the bench for a discussion, and when Harris resumed his questioning, he chose to seek a summary.

"Clarence, did these people say anything to you about any of your rights?" he asked, to which Tucker simply replied, "No, sir."

His version of the interrogations continued through the detectives' handful of "tickets," and questions about various crimes in Cincinnati. Then Harris turned to the significant point of the original trial.

"Now during this entire investigation," he asked, "did you ever make this statement to any of your interrogators: 'Well, we bought the gun. We had a stolen car and didn't intend to let anyone take us in custody.' Did you make that statement?"

"I did not make that statement," Tucker responded. He again described threats made by the Cincinnati officers and admitted to the burglary of the hotel. He repeated that two reporters were present during the interrogation.

"Did you see the newspaper article?" Harris queried. "Did it accurately represent what had transpired at the interrogation?"

"Yes, just as I recalled it," Tucker said.

"It made no mention of you participating in any way in the shooting incident?"

"No, sir."

Tucker continued, with Harris's prompting, to describe the second interrogation, during which ex-Chief Cornwell and Prosecutor Shoup alternately sought a confession of conspiracy from Tucker while editing the transcription by clerk Dorothy McFadden. Tucker repeated that he was never informed of constitutional rights, nor asked about representation by counsel. And he was "thoroughly confused. But the two asking questions at the same time made matters worse."

"Did they do this in the form of questions, or accusations?" Harris asked. "What did they say to you?"

"'You boys bought this gun to do this. You planned this a long time ago,'" Tucker recalled. "I told them no. Shoup would become hysterical, and Cornwell would start hollering at me."

Tucker then described the session witnessed briefly by his uncle Neal, and he repeated that up to that point he had not consulted with anyone—"no attorney, no friend, no relative, nobody."

"When was the first time you saw an attorney?" Harris asked.

"The morning after I pled not guilty."

"You were brought into court without an attorney?" Harris said, "and you pled not guilty to the incident without an attorney?"

Tucker replied, "That is right."

With further questioning by Harris, Tucker described his living arrangements before the trial. He slept on a board, he said, and although eventually he was given relative freedom of movement in the cell area during daylight hours, he was isolated from all other prisoners. Deputies closely monitored his meetings with relatives, Tucker testified, and he recalled the episode in which his stepmother mentioned the trial "and my father and her were hustled out. The interview was ended there."

Harris now steered the testimony in the direction of Tucker's court-appointed defense. "Let's talk a little about your relations with your court-appointed counsel. Who was it?" he asked.

"There was an uncle and a nephew," Tucker said.

"Did you discuss with your counsel anything concerning the feelings in the area and if the case should be tried in the county?"

"They told me about the feelings in the county and insisted we couldn't get a jury who would give us a favorable verdict or a just one, so therefore they should waive a jury trial."

"Did they discuss having a jury in another county?"

"No sir. Not with me."

"Do you recall if your counsel discussed whether you and Evans should be tried together or separately?"

"They mentioned it one time," Tucker replied, "but they said they couldn't do a thing about it because the prosecutor wanted them tried together."

"Did you discuss with your counsel whether or not you would testify yourself at the trial?" Harris continued. "Did you want to testify?"

"No, sir, not really," Tucker said. "I realized it would have hurt Evans. It would have been direct testimony against him. The way things set, I didn't feel it necessary."

"The court-appointed attorneys went along with that?" Harris questioned.

"They kept telling me they were moving for an acquittal for me and felt it would be granted. I believed."

Harris turned briefly to the issue of the reporters who witnessed the initial interrogation. He asked Tucker if, during the trial, the defense team sought those reporters for testimony.

"I said we should find out who they are," Tucker replied. "He said there was no way to find out who they were. He said it wouldn't be any use."

Harris punctuated his session with one final question for Tucker. "I'm going to ask you once again: Did you ever say to anyone that you and Evans had an agreement to shoot it out with the police and not be taken in?"

"I never said that," an obviously exhausted Tucker snapped emphatically.

Chapter 13

::

By this time, Tucker had been on the witness stand all morning. Judge Aultman, seeing that Tucker obviously was drained, called a brief recess, perhaps to give the plaintiff a few moments to revive himself.

Then "Johnny" Neatherton, known for his longish wavy hair and impeccable suits, began his cross-examination, asking first about Tucker's friendship with Evans, and about their homes in Cincinnati. The Kemper Lane Hotel burglary was recounted, again, and then Neatherton turned to the pair's plan to go north.

"Then you went to Ravenna?" Neatherton asked.

"We didn't leave right away, no, sir," Tucker replied. "There was a day or two there. Then Evans got this drunken idea of seeing this girlfriend he knew up there."

Neatherton's purpose was then revealed. "Did you have a gun of any type when you left Cincinnati, or when you were at the Kemper Lane Hotel?" Harris jumped in immediately, trying to head off the gun talk, a dangerous area for Tucker. "I object," he said, "not only on the grounds of irrelevancy, but on the grounds that these are matters not gone into on direct examination."

Judge Aultman was not persuaded. "Overruled," he responded. Then Tucker admitted the two boys "had an old broken-down shotgun, an old, old thing. It belonged to my grandfather, when usable I guess you'd say."

"Are you stating it wouldn't work?"

"Well," Tucker said, "let's say this: It's been years since I've seen that gun, but I would not fire it, even twenty years ago, twenty-one years ago."

"You had it along for appearance?"

"It was broken. I was going to have it repaired and use it for rabbit hunting later."

"It was just an irrational thing?" a dubious Neatherton asked.

The prosecutor asked about the source of the revolver used by Evans, but Harris again objected, and was overruled again. "Then you purchased the gun?" Neatherton asked. "What was the purpose in purchasing this weapon?"

Harris once again objected, "on all grounds available." Once again, the judge disagreed. Neatherton, tiring of the interruptions, suggested that he would recognize Harris had a continuing objection to the line of questioning. He again turned to Tucker.

"The price on that thing was thirty-some dollars, half the value of the same weapon in Cincinnati," Tucker said. "Now, like I say on the shotgun, it's been twenty-one years, but I remember the ejector mechanism would not work. He pointed that out to me and said that is why it was so cheap. The ejector mechanism was worn and wouldn't push the empty shells out."

"Why did you buy it?"

"Just a good buy. I figured to resell the thing. It was worth double the amount I paid for it."

"Were you looking for bargains in guns in Ravenna?" Neatherton asked.

"No, sir. It happened to be there. If it had been a radio at half price, I would have bought the radio and doubled my money," Tucker said.

"You weren't a gun collector, or anything like that?" Neatherton asked. Then he changed the subject to the boys' transportation, and Tucker volunteered that the pair had used a stolen automobile to get to Ravenna, which he described as thirty-five miles from Cleveland. More Neatherton questions led Tucker to explain the disposition of the original Buick: "Evans shot holes in the gas tank and set it on fire somewhere between Akron and Cleveland."

"What did you do for transportation then?" Neatherton asked.

"We stole another car," Tucker answered.

Neatherton jumped at that response. "You say 'we.' You and Mr. Evans were in this together?"

"Yes, sir."

Harris interrupted with an objection. "Irrelevant and not on direct and all other grounds," he said; Tucker went on. "We lived in Cincinnati and wanted to get home."

"Was that the car you had in Xenia?"

"There was one in between there. There were three cars involved."

"Three stolen cars?" Neatherton continued.

"Yes."

Neatherton recalled that Tucker had said earlier that the gun used by Evans was in their car's glove box.

Tucker agreed, reiterating that it was unloaded. If Evans didn't have time to load the gun when he reached into the Buick to extinguish its lights, Neatherton asked, "When was it loaded?"

"Some time after I put it in the glove compartment. It was unloaded and in the holster, snaps fastened down, the last time I handled it. Evans had handled it after that."

"All right, sir," Neatherton continued. "During this time, you were confined at the county jail. Did you ever ask for an attorney over there?"

"To be honest with you," Tucker replied, "I was afraid to ask for anything."

Neatherton asked Tucker to explain when he and his court-appointed attorneys had been able to meet. Tucker said most of their discussion took place at the table during the trial.

"How many days did the trial last, as near as you remember?" Neatherton asked.

"Three."

Neatherton continued, "They consulted with you, if you wanted to take the stand?"

"They asked how I felt about it."

"Do you remember when Mr. Cornwell was on the stand?" the attorney questioned.

"Yes."

"I would like to refresh your memory and refer to—I'm reading from the transcript. This is Mr. Cornwell speaking: 'I cautioned him as to his rights under the Constitution of the United States, and it was not required he testify against himself, and he told me he was willing to make a complete statement. We sent for Mrs. McFadden, the court steno.' Do you recall that testimony? Is it a true statement?" he asked of Tucker.

"I disagree with it. He did not advise me of constitutional rights or that it would be used against me. The way that happened is the way I testified. They asked my version, and they were very unhappy with it."

The prosecuting attorney ended his time with the witness by asking if family members had visited Tucker, and whether his uncle had testified at the trial. Tucker described the closely monitored meetings with his family members, and said his uncle Neal had come into the courtroom, but the Smiths "signaled for him to leave. They didn't want to use him as a witness."

Harris returned and asked Tucker to clarify the purchase of the pistol. "Do you recall whether this was a sporting goods store, or pawn shop, or what?" he asked.

"It was a sporting goods store," Tucker said. "I remember that so well because we went to buy a model airplane." He confirmed that he had bought the airplane.

Neatherton responded with his own questions about the Ravenna store incident, and heard Tucker describe the purchase of the gun, holster, and 119 rounds of ammunition as "a package deal. This all went with it." With that, Tucker was allowed to leave the witness stand.

He was replaced there by his father, Earl "Popeye" Tucker, who under questioning by Harris described his difficulties in trying to visit his son and the "hostile" attitudes of the jail staff. He added his discussions with "Foss" Hopkins, but testimony was halted when Neatherton objected to it as hearsay.

Harris then turned his attention to the local newspaper. He asked that copies of articles published in *The Evening Gazette*, renamed the *Xenia Daily Gazette*, be placed in evidence. After some discussion, and a half-hour recess, he called the editor and general manager, Jack Jordan, to the stand.

Tucker, with Sheriff's Deputy, meets *Xenia Daily Gazette* Editor Jack Jordan during the 1967 hearing (Photo courtesy of Greene County Public Library Greene Room--Local History and Genealogy, Xenia, Ohio)

Jordan, a large man with a commanding voice, a bulbous face, and a generous shock of graying hair, described the geographic circulation of *The Gazette* in 1946 as "within the confines of Greene County, with a slight overlap at that time basically to the south." With that comment, the editor was dismissed from the stand, and after a brief discussion among the lawyers and Aultman at the bench, the hearing was recessed for lunch.

Jordan remained in the courtroom, however, because he had a special relationship with the case, and Tucker. He had been *The Gazette* reporter who covered the case in 1946, and he took the liberty of interviewing the prisoner during the recess to record his fascination with the changes he saw in Tucker after twenty-one years.

"He remembered me, but not as well as I remembered him," Jordan wrote in a *Gazette* column the following day. "My recollection is one of a frightened young man in hostile surroundings."

"As Tucker testified in his hearing, it was apparent that nearly twenty-one years of incarceration had not been wasted," Jordan continued. "He expressed himself well, his vocabulary was good. Here was a man, sent away as a boy, who has improved himself."

Jordan reported that he had asked if Tucker was optimistic about his chances for freedom after the hearing. "I'm keeping my fingers crossed," Tucker replied. "You might keep yours crossed for me, too."

At 1:00 p.m., the hearing reconvened, with Tucker now dressed in a white sweater, white shirt, dark tie, and dress slacks. "It's the first time I've worn civies in twenty years and nine months," he commented.

Jordan observed that the new apparel pleased and brightened the attitude of the prisoner. "He wore a broad grin at reference to his improved attire," Jordan wrote, "and even kidded his father for ribbing him."

Judge Aultman invited Harris to make his summary statement. "Your honor," Harris began, "it is apparent from the transcript, the petition, the files, and the records in the original proceedings, and from the testimony presented this morning, that in order to find this petitioner guilty of murder in the first-degree, there must have been a conclusive finding that he acted as co-conspirator with the one who did the actual killing of Sheriff Confer.

"The events and circumstances by Ernest Evans, as testified to in the transcript by Officer Anderson, when taken alone, can in no way support the conviction of Clarence Tucker," Harris continued. "They proffer this petitioner did not participate; he made no effort to flee or escape arrest; he made no effort to aid Evans though requested to do so; and both officers were wounded and helpless on the ground. The petitioner stood by with his arms in the air."

"By no stretch of the imagination could such convict Clarence Tucker," Harris observed.

"Now, Your Honor," he continued, "the feeling was understandably high against the petitioner and Evans immediately after this occurrence. But despite the horrendousness of the crime, the essential question this Court must answer at this time, was there a denial or infringement of the rights of the petitioner as would render the judgment void or voidable under the Constitution of Ohio and the United States?"

Having established the foundation of his post-conviction remedy petition, Harris turned to the particulars of the case. "The prosecutor was aware of the weakness of the case against Tucker," Harris explained to the courtroom. "The only way he could obtain a conviction was to obtain his confession to the effect he had conspired not to be taken, but to shoot it out with any officer trying to apprehend them.

"It is the involuntariness that infringes most heavily on the rights of this petitioner," Harris observed. "The law of Ohio has always been the accused must be warned of his right to counsel and his right to remain silent," Harris said, and he then reviewed what he described as "a few discrepancies in the testimony." The attorney noted that a reporter and photographer attended the first interrogation session and wrote a story without a word of conspiracy theory presented. "This reporter, even then, was good enough to know a conspiracy confession is a good story," Harris commented.

Further, interrogation by Cornwell and Shoup was not completely recorded, Harris added, and then the prosecutor didn't ask Tucker to sign the transcription. "Why did the prosecutor hesitate in asking the defendant to sign?" Harris asked rhetorically. "The transcribed portion does not contain admission of conspiracy to shoot it out with the law."

Harris reserved Cornwell's version of the questioning for special scorn. "Mr. Cornwell's testimony falls apart," he suggested. "There is nothing there that will support a confession." To support his observation, Harris read portions of the transcript in which Cornwell tried to remember statements that Tucker was asked to confirm.

"This went on and on," Harris said. "During the interrogation, he referred to the defendant trying to answer some of the questions, but Shoup would ask a question at the same time Cornwell asked, and the defendant started getting confused and sat and shrugged his shoulders." The entire session resulted in "this purported confession that sent the defendant to prison for twenty years," Harris said in a huff.

"I know that as early as 1953, when I first had contact with this case," Harris said, "I received a letter from Mr. Clarence Tucker, which had the same stipulations as testified to here today, and at no time during all of these proceedings has his story wavered one iota. It has been consistently true, and I believe it."

He noted that the interrogations by Shoup and Cornwell took place on January 29, but the lead article of *The Evening Gazette* the next day indicated Shoup had not decided how to charge Tucker.

"So on the morning following testimony of a positive confession, the prosecutor still was not sure what he was going to charge this petitioner with," Harris observed. "And I claim, Your Honor, this is positively contradictory. Any prosecutor, if he had this confession, would have charged the way he wanted to charge and not have to interview more witnesses."

At this point, Harris employed the supporting precedent. "Your Honor, we submit this is precisely the type of overzealousness which the Supreme Court of the United States has condemned in holding a prisoner, as in Davis v. North Carolina," he said. "The Court found that Davis went through a prolonged period of police interrogation, and we submit such an atmosphere occurred here."

"This boy, without counsel, with a ninth-grade education, held under a convenient charge of suspicion without access to newspapers for fourteen days, not taken before a magistrate or a judge, not yet indicted of any criminal act, not brought before any judge for preliminary hearing, not charged with any crime, was interrogated extensively over a several day period by skilled investigators. He would have had to be steeped in the knowledge of the law to know that he could be charged with murder in the first-degree for what his companion, not he, did; but what Clarence didn't know, his interrogators fully understood that it is necessary, in order to obtain a joint conviction, a conspiracy be definitely shown. To this end, the defendant's constitutional rights were violated."

"In this record, we have no signed unequivocal confession, but only the verbal recollections of a group of police officers, rightfully righteously outraged over the killing of one of their brethren and wounding of another. It is well-settled if conspiracy is an element, it must be proven beyond a reasonable doubt."

Harris noted that failure to notify the prisoner of his rights to silence and representation by an attorney met the tests of the Miranda and Escobedo cases. He added that those decisions had a "retroactive effect" because the High Court included language that "past defendants may still avail themselves of the involuntariness test."

Having established his major argument, Harris turned to "a number of secondary grounds which are not a great matter but nonetheless serious." First, he said, Tucker was denied the right of separate trial. Further, the defendant was not given a change of venue, or even the opportunity to make that request, despite "numerous newspaper articles for all to hear prior to its being testified to at trial."

"The petitioner's life was at stake, public opinion was so prejudiced, feeling so high, because of the heinousness of the crime, and we admit it is inconceivable your petitioner could have been afforded a fair trial. The three-judge panel, on its own motion, should have transferred this to another county where the defendant could have made a fair determination as to whether to stake his life on a jury or three judges."

Lastly, Harris accused the defense team of mounting a halfhearted defense. Even after Tucker's conviction, he said, the Smiths declined to attempt an appeal, incorrectly guessing the severity of Tucker's penalty.

"Your Honor, in summing up, this petitioner has served over twenty years in the Ohio State Penitentiary," Harris concluded. "Clarence Tucker may not have been a good boy or a good citizen, but he was not convicted of being a bad boy or a bad citizen, or being a liquor thief, or of being a car thief. He was convicted of murder, and he is not a murderer.

"Your Honor, this boy has served twenty years of his life in prison for a crime which he did not perpetrate. He is like a bird in your hand today. You can crush his hopes, and with that, you crush him, or you can open your hands and allow him to go free."

Harris concluded with, "I believe Clarence Tucker deserves that freedom."

Neatherton's simple response paled in comparison to Harris's carefully manicured prose. "We weren't here twenty years ago and can't pass on the actions of counsel at that time," he began, offering praise for "the abilities of George Smith as an attorney before this bar." Harris had cherry-picked the weakest parts of that defense, Neatherton said, so he would do the same. He said he was bothered by Tucker's weak excuse for buying the revolver, "because it was a good buy," and confused by Tucker's narration of his interrogations.

Neatherton agreed that the Supreme Court's Escobedo and Miranda cases assured the defendants' rights, even retroactively. "Did they have them twenty years ago?" he asked. "I think they did. I think the record is clear. The impassive part Tucker played—I think twenty years is sufficient time. He has paid for the part he's done, but even that would have no bearing on what the circumstances were twenty years ago.

"The fact does remain," the prosecutor noted, "they were in a stolen car."

That led Neatherton to focus on a defense of police activity. "They were advised of their rights, I'm certain," he said, adding a reservation. "I have no argument with Mr. Harris that some of these things were not done, but were those same conditions existing twenty years ago?"

Neatherton suggested perhaps Cornwell was overzealous as well, but Cornwell wasn't working at that time for Greene County in any capacity. Mezger and Schath's team tactics didn't surprise him, either, but by his reading of the transcript they, too, had advised Tucker of his constitutional rights.

"I'm not saying these officers were so far-sighted twenty years ago to know the questions they asked or the advice they gave would stand up to the light of recent Supreme Court decisions, but as I understand this post-conversion statute, what was the law at that time?"

"I can only say I am glad that this is your decision, not mine," Neatherton concluded.

Judge Aultman adjourned the court at 2:05 p.m. At the conclusion of the statements, he explained that because of the complex laws involved, his decision would take a few days. He would render a judgment then, he said. Tucker was returned to Columbus to await the decision.

The "few days" Tucker had to wait turned into months. Perhaps because he was forced to examine the merits of a decision made by my father, his good friend, Dan Aultman mulled the merits of Harris's arguments for eight months.

Earl Tucker filled the interval with a job in the Ohio Penitentiary records office, but he later recalled those days as excruciating. The period between the hearing and Aultman's decision seemed as long as the score of years he already had endured, he told a reporter. He couldn't know whether, after twenty-one years, he would have to stand trial again, linger in prison four more years until his next parole board hearing, or be set free.

Chapter 14

::

Late in the afternoon of Thursday, October 12, 1967, reporter Bob Burns of the *Xenia Daily Gazette* telephoned Warden E.L. Maxwell of the Ohio State Penitentiary. A Greene County judge had just revealed a decision, Burns told the warden. Clarence Earl Tucker had been granted a new trial; trying a long shot, Burns asked the warden if he could talk to Tucker on the telephone. The warden took the telephone number of the *Gazette* reporter and agreed to call back in a few minutes, which the warden did, fifteen minutes later. "He said, 'That's wonderful! I'm real happy to hear it,'" Maxwell reported. "Tucker said he knows the decision means he gets out." Burns, a smallish, quiet fellow and not an especially aggressive reporter, nevertheless repeated his request to speak directly to Tucker, who was working in the records office when he was notified. "That's against prison policy," Burns was told.

The next day, Friday, October 13, Judge Aultman formally released his findings in the matter of Ohio v. Tucker. In a five-page document, he summarized Tucker's testimony and the seven arguments of the petition, hinting at his decision early by observing that "the defendant was questioned intermittently by various officials; in the opinion of the court he was not effectively warned of his absolute constitutional right to remain silent, nor did he intelligently waive his right to counsel."

Judge Aultman didn't spare my father, Judge Frank Johnson, or the other members of the tribunal. "In view of the recent Court decision," Judge Aultman concluded, "it is the duty of the trial Court in considering whether a confession was voluntary or involuntary, to examine the entire record, and it was not done in this case." Aultman added that legal safeguards against making such an involuntary confession had been preserved in the recent court cases, so claims could be retroactive.

"Therefore, in consideration of the interrogation of the Defendant Tucker, the Court is of the opinion that substantial coercive influence was brought to bear upon the defendant, and therefore, the incriminating statements made by the Defendant against himself were a violation of his constitutional rights."

For Judge Aultman, this was sufficient. "It will be unnecessary to pass on the other grounds set forth in the Defendant's position," he wrote. "The Court will, therefore, set aside the sentence imposed upon the Defendant," Judge Aultman concluded, "and grant the Defendant a new trial."

The following Monday, Judge Aultman signed the entry ordering Tucker to be "released from the confines of the Ohio State Penitentiary forthwith," but it wasn't to be for renewed testimony in court. Marshall Peterson, the prosecuting attorney in Greene County, had decided enough was enough. He explained to the *Xenia Daily Gazette* that justice had been served, and a new trial could not even be considered because of the time lapse since the crime occurred.

"We'll do all that we can to see that Tucker has a speedy release," said Peterson. "It should be just a matter of days," he surmised.

Just over forty-eight hours later, a prison clerk scribbled "10-19-67 Sentence vacated by Com Pleas Ct. Greene Cty. To Sheriff Greene County" into the great book Tucker had signed twenty-one years, nine months, and nineteen days earlier. Still in custody, Tucker rode through a rainy day back to Xenia with Greene County Probation Officers John Thomas and John Baxley.

"Man, am I glad to be out of there," Tucker exclaimed as he climbed out of the police cruiser at the Greene County jail, where he had to wait overnight to sign the final papers. When he was booked, a *Xenia Daily Gazette* photographer captured the image of a slightly wrinkled Tucker, now with a receding hairline, flashing a broad, toothy grin. He recalled his social security number quite flawlessly, but stumbled when asked his occupation. "I wouldn't know what to put down," he said.

A smiling Clarence Earl Tucker signs documents ending 21 years in prison. (Photo courtesy of Greene County Public Library Greene Room--Local History and Genealogy, Xenia, Ohio)

The photo was printed the following day, when delightfully warm, clear autumn weather greeted Tucker, wearing a green sport coat and tie, as he hobbled to the court offices in his characteristic unsteady gait. In a brief four-minute hearing, Judge Herman Weber, serving for the vacationing Judge Aultman, accepted the prosecutor's "Nolle Prosequi" document, meaning the county chose not to pursue Tucker's murder indictment. Then, Judge Weber ended case number 8101 as it pertained to defendant Clarence Tucker by signing a simple entry: "For good cause shown, the defendant is ordered released forthwith."

Tucker left the court building that day, past maple trees with orange-tinted leaves on the courthouse lawn, trees that had been mere saplings when Tucker first took that walk. "What can a man say? I'm dumbfounded, speechless," Tucker said to reporters.

Now, something of a local media celebrity, Tucker told a *Gazette* reporter in an interview that he would soon leave with his uncle Neal for Cincinnati, where he would live with his father, who was by this time sixty-five years old. "A fellow who hired me when I was a kid of twenty has offered me a job," he said. But it's in electronics, something I don't know much about."

"I want to go to work and drop out of sight and stay out of everybody's hair," he added.

With that, Tucker climbed into Neal's car with *Dayton Daily News* reporter Henry Saeman, who had been following Tucker's case since the hearing in February. The car rolled south to Cincinnati, not on the two-lane roads Tucker had used twenty-one years before, but on the new four-lane Interstate 75. En route, Tucker expressed fascination with the autumn colors and Southwest Ohio's rolling countryside.

His family still lived at the same Bishop Street apartment, so when Tucker arrived, he instinctively retraced his limping steps down the dark hallway to their lower-level walkout flat. His father stood waiting in its doorway, outlined by the lights within. But when his middle-aged son approached, wearing a sport coat and tie, Popeye said nothing. He appeared not to recognize the man who stood before him. Over twenty years, Popeye had grown used to seeing Earl in prison denim.

The newly freed Clarence Earl Tucker joins his father "Popeye" and the family dog in their apartment (Photo courtesy of Wright State University, the *Dayton Daily News* Archives)

The pair stood in wordless silence. Then they shook hands. Earl "Popeye" Tucker and his namesake, Clarence Earl Tucker, turned and walked into the kitchen, where Popeye's big dog sniffed at the new family member.

"I'm tired," the new arrival said.

: :

Two days before he departed Ohio Penitentiary forever, Tucker encountered his old friend Ernie Evans in a prison hallway. Both men were "lifers"—sentenced to spend their lives behind the prison walls—whose exceptional twenty-one-year records had earned them honor status. But now Tucker had heard that he would walk out, a free man. Evans could hardly mask his heartache. "Glad to see you made it," was all he could mutter at the news.

Since his near-death experience in 1949, Evans had remained an obscure, well-mannered inmate, but in parole sessions, he heard the same disappointments that Tucker had. By tradition, the Parole Board would not grant a commutation for cop killers, and the governor would not grant clemency without a Parole Board recommendation. Nor would he get any help from Tucker's legal team: when Tucker's attorneys met with Joe Anderson, the deputy said he would support the appeal by Tucker, but not one for Evans, the incident's triggerman.

Nevertheless, by the 1960s, Evans's exemplary behavior earned for him an extraordinary opportunity. Since the postwar administration of Ohio Governor C. William O'Neill, the state's chief executive had lived with his family in Bexley, a Columbus suburb, in a twenty-five-room mansion that the Rev. Charles Harris had deeded to the state in the mid-1950s. To maintain the substantial house and grounds, Ohio followed the example of other states with executive mansions, acquiring the services of inmates from the state penitentiary.

The practice of using prison labor at the mansion fascinated O'Neill's successor, Michael V. DiSalle, who described the residence as "a pile of mongrel architecture with a fieldstone and half-timbered exterior." Throughout his term in office, DiSalle sifted among capital cases and clemency requests with unease, to the extent that he authored a book examining his experience with capital punishment in Ohio. In his writing, he recalled five inmates with murder convictions who stayed at the mansion, either on the third floor or above the garage, and the remainder who were transported daily from the penitentiary. "They were yardmen, gardeners, chauffeurs, housemen, laundrymen, cooks, and handymen.... All had access to the Mansion at all times—the refrigerator if they were hungry at night; the kitchen and the downstairs recreation room to receive their relatives and other visitors on weekends."

The chosen inmates—"homicidal housemen" and "murderous domestics," DiSalle called them—were acquired through a program called the Ohio Lifer's Hope Law, under which the sentences of prisoners serving life terms would be reviewed after twenty years. Prison officials would examine the records of eligible inmates and recommend those with appropriate behavior for work at the mansion. "Here, they could be observed by the governor who would make the final decision," wrote DiSalle, who noted that during this term of evaluation, many of these men became well-acquainted with members of the state's First Family.

"It was a plum position to have," explained Michal Mainwaring, whose father served as Registrar of Motor Vehicles in the next administration, that of James A.

Rhodes, and who herself worked in state government. "They earned that position. By the time anybody was chosen to work there, they were exemplary prisoners."

"The people who were around the Governor's Mansion would get to know these guys by their first names, and all their stories. It was redemptive."

One of the inmates thus redeemed was Ernie Evans, according to Tucker's attorney Irving Harris, who counted Governor Rhodes among his Columbus friends. Harris said that Evans became a part of the trustee team working at the Governor's Mansion during Rhodes' first term. The always-affable Evans became so familiar with the governor, Harris reported, that he played pool with Rhodes and the governor's friends.

"They would come over every day in a van," remembered Sue Moore, the daughter of Rhodes who, as a teenager, lived part-time in the Bexley Mansion while attending The Ohio State University. "The van would pick them up and take them back at the end of the day. There was a pool table in the basement. My dad would go down to the basement and say that while they were waiting they could play pool."

"Dad probably had his pajamas on," Moore recalled with a laugh. "He'd come home from work and put on his pajamas. He was a people person—easy to talk to."

Moore recalls that the group of about a dozen inmates—"every one was a first-degree murderer," she said—took their work seriously. "Their supervisor was really strict. They really toed the line when he was around."

The hard work could have immense benefits, however. In both the DiSalle and Rhodes administrations, if, after this period of evaluation, the governor was satisfied of an inmate's rehabilitation, it was the practice of the governor to pardon the inmate. So naturally, when word arrived of Tucker's release, Evans made sure that his friend, the governor, knew about it.

Evans was raking leaves near the mansion driveway one day late that fall when the governor arrived. Still brash and confident as ever, Evans interrupted his work and walked over to Rhodes. "Mr. Governor, sir, could I have a moment of your time?" he asked.

"Sure, son. What can I do for you?" Rhodes replied.

"Well, sir, I've been in for twenty-one years. And I just found out my buddy, who went in the same time I did, well, he just got his release."

"I was wondering, Mr. Governor, could you look into my case for me, maybe help me out, too?"

"You a lifer?" Rhodes asked, although he really knew the answer.

"Yessir." Evans gripped the handle of his leaf rake firmly and held it instinctively in front of himself, as if to hide behind it.

"Your buddy wasn't one of this crew, was he?"

"No, sir. He got a lawyer and went to court."

"Hmm. That's so? Well, I'll see what we can do," Rhodes said. He smiled broadly, reached up, and slapped Evans on the back. "Ernie, right? We'll see."

"Thank you, sir."

Rhodes was as good as his word although, as was typical of his approach to clemency cases, his name was omitted even though his influence prevailed. As the result of an application filed by Evans before the Parole Board's meeting of December 8, 1967, the Board voted to reduce Evans's conviction to second-degree murder, but the Board's 5-2 vote indicated some unease among its members. They stated, "The inmate's accomplice was released by vacation of sentence Oct. 19, 1967." The Board observed in its remarks, "The inmate's own institutional record is of such excellence as to assure that he can be released on parole without risk to society."

A few days later, a clerk in the Ohio Penitentiary added in the big book a new notation at the name of Ernest Finley Evans, No. 83750 Murder 1st Deg. (mercy). "12-12-67 Commutation of sentence by Gov. Rhodes for murder 1st Deg. to Murder 2nd Deg.

"12-22-67 Paroled."

Chapter 15

::

Clarence Earl Tucker and his uncle Neal had been surrounded by a cluster of reporters after all the papers had been signed in the Greene County Courthouse, and several had the same question: Did the man now freed after twenty-one years of prison feel any bitterness toward the State?

"I got that out of my system a long time ago," Tucker replied. "Bitterness eats you up inside. There has been enough heartache connected with this case."

"Is there any possibility," one reporter asked, "that Clarence would ever return to Xenia for a visit?"

"No, I don't think so," Neal replied, with emphasis. "Just too many bad memories here."

With that, the Tuckers turned their backs on Xenia, presumably forever. Earl Tucker went home to Cincinnati and took the job he had been promised in a television repair shop, but he found little satisfaction in that. After a while, he turned to working with wood, a craft he enjoyed. In fine carpentry and cabinet-making, Tucker finally found a calling.

Then the troubles began. At one job after another, someone would recognize him, or discover his full name. "Say, aren't you Clarence Tucker, the ex-con cop killer?" was the question he began to dread. Formerly friendly neighbors would begin to look away; customers would ask for references, then disappear; and employers would ask him to gather his tools and leave.

In his mind, Earl Tucker had been exonerated. He thought Judge Aultman's court in October 1967, had separated him from Clarence Tucker, the boy who had been unjustly imprisoned for so many years. Yet the pain continued. Clarence Tucker the arrest victim wouldn't fade away, even as years passed.

In that time, as he pondered his situation, he realized Irving Harris's preparation for the hearing had identified several factors that infringed on his rights. These were the interrogations he endured, the lack of adequate legal representation, and the prejudicial news coverage. Among all of these, no one person remained to whom Tucker could address his continuing grievances. No one, except Jack Jordan of the *Xenia Daily Gazette*, who had reported on the original trial in 1946 and then interviewed Tucker at the 1967 hearing. Jordan's articles of thirty years before, exposed in the hearing as a source that had caused grief for Clarence Tucker, continued to exist.

So, in 1977, Tucker traveled back to Xenia to clear his name, literally, once and for all. He rented unit number nine in a trailer court on North Detroit Street and called Jack Jordan to explain that *The Gazette* should revisit the story it had covered thirty-one years before. Jordan, no doubt dumbfounded by the request, referred Tucker to his executive editor, Delores Fisher. In several meetings and phone conversations, Tucker explained that his past continued to haunt him because he was being remembered as Clarence Tucker, the boy found guilty in Xenia for a murder he did not commit. He wanted his good name back, he said, and *The Gazette* could do that by correcting its faulty coverage of the 1946 trial.

Of course, *The Gazette* editors declined to devote resources to such a scheme. A frustrated Tucker then turned to the only option he could afford, a one-inch ad he wrote and had placed in *The Gazette* personals for a week, from January 26 to January 30, 1978. It read:

> *Earl Tucker hereby gives notice that a lawsuit will follow any further personal, financial or property damage or destruction by any person or persons maintaining he has ever voluntarily used any name other than the one recorded on the date of his birth as his name. No further comment is necessary, except in court.*

Tucker followed that message with a terse memo and letter to Jordan, in which he expended all his options. "A newspaper is a powerful weapon even when it is used to shovel manure, and that is exactly what your '*Evening Gazette*' was used for in 1946," he wrote. "The much publicised (*sic*) alleged policy of *The Gazette* to retract false information and publish the truth is either just some more nonsense or it isn't."

"I don't have anything to hide," he continued, "but the falsehoods in *The Evening Gazette* have played hell with me for more than thirty years. Isn't that enough?"

In a formal letter that accompanied the memo, Tucker said he wanted to go over the content piece by piece, so Jordan would understand why the original stories of 1946 should be retracted. His complaints amounted to relatively routine errors that would occur in deadline reporting: a gun with five chambers for bullets, not six; a stop by deputies who followed Tucker's car for two blocks, hardly the "chase" reported in the paper; and a disagreement about the factual accuracy of waiter Doug James's trial testimony.

To fix the errors, Tucker submitted his own sparse two-paragraph account of the event the morning of January 29, 1946. In factual content, it actually differed little from contemporary reports, although he included commentary maintaining there had never been a confession of conspiracy, and the pair of youths had indeed been denied the opportunity to sufficiently defend themselves in court.

"What would be so wrong with some responsible journalism regarding that case?" Tucker asked. "A pretty rotten thing was perpetrated here in Greene County against the driver of that car in 1946, but you know that."

Tucker added that he believed he had been indicted and convicted because he refused to testify against Evans "with statements that Clarence Tucker was instructed to make in a courtroom. Somebody didn't want any truth in that courtroom."

"The honest facts of that case are not a black eye to Clarence Tucker," wrote the alter ego, Earl Tucker. "The man police identified as Clarence Tucker was never guilty of anything whatsoever in Greene County, Ohio, in 1946 or any other time."

Tucker concluded his missive by repeating his threat of legal action and describing his state of exasperation. "The personal, financial, and property destruction that I have endured because of that case against Clarence Tucker has gone far enough," he wrote. "All I have to do is attempt to establish myself and be doing well, when some sneak will appear with misinformation and my every positive endeavor towards living a decent life will be utterly destroyed."

But the *Xenia Daily Gazette* didn't accept his proposed manuscript, didn't revisit the old story nor run a retraction. Within a year, Earl Tucker vacated his trailer on North Detroit Street, and vanished from Xenia.

Epilogue

::

On Sunday, June 1, 1997 Greene County Prosecutor William F. Schenck gave the keynote address dedicating a memorial to honor Deputy Earl Confer and five other law officers who had given their lives in the service of the county. There was a proclamation by the County Commission and a 21-gun salute. To this day, the site at the Xenia F.O.P Lodge on Dayton-Xenia Road, about halfway between the courthouse and the old infirmary, remains notable for its six cabernet-colored granite blocks placed there, one for each name, looking much like neat headstones.

The man who caused the name of Earl Confer to be among those so honored left Ohio Penitentiary at Christmas time in 1967 and found a job as an engineering technician with the Ohio Department of Highways. Ernest Finley Evans soon married, began a family, and bought a pleasant house in a suburban neighborhood typical of the time.

Almost exactly eight years after his release from prison, the morning of December 8, 1975, Evans died of a massive heart attack. He was fifty years and five months old at the time, and he was buried in a nearby cemetery. His widow kept their house for many years, according to county records.

::

The girl Ernie Evans dreamed of marrying during World War II, and whose memory prompted his trip to Northeast Ohio in January 1946, returned home after his trial that spring and completed her cosmetology training. June Marie Edwards let Ernie pass out of her life, although according to June, her sister Ruthie and husband Ed Raskov did travel to Columbus to visit Ernie in prison once. June never saw Ernie Evans again after the trial, and a few years later, she married and had two sons and two daughters—all of whom stayed in the Ravenna area, while June enjoyed a successful career as a field representative with the Ohio Commission on Aging. One of her sons, Marty Hill, became one of the most successful high school basketball coaches in Ohio history.

::

Marcus Shoup, the Greene County prosecuting attorney who subpoenaed Junie Evans in 1946, was shortly thereafter elected president of the Prosecuting Attorneys Association of Ohio. He emphasized that experience during what was described as "spirited campaigning" in the Republican primary election of May 1948, but lost in results that *The Evening Gazette* proclaimed as an upset. The victor, by 491 votes out of just over 6,000 cast, was Judge Dan Aultman's 32-year-old brother Philip Aultman, the only World War II veteran in the slate of Republicans.

The defeated Shoup returned to the practice of law as a senior partner of the firm Shoup & Hagler. He lived in the same residence where he had been born, at 158 East Main Street in Xenia, until he died unexpectedly at age 69, in November 1971. Upon his death, Greene County's judges interrupted their court schedules for official memorial services in the county courtrooms.

: :

Judge Dan Aultman, brother of the man who defeated Shoup in the 1948 primaries, succeeded my father as judge of the Greene County Common Pleas Court in 1955. He was re-elected to the bench in 1956, 1962, 1968, and 1974, and during his nearly quarter-century tenure as judge, he was honored by both the Republican Party and the Ohio Supreme Court. He retired in 1978 to attend to his award-winning chicken farming full-time, but two years later, at age 73, he died in his car while en route home from a community meeting.

: :

Irving Harris, the attorney who argued for Clarence Earl Tucker's release in the court of Judge Aultman, became a successful lawyer in Cincinnati with the firm Cors, Hair & Hartsock (authors' note: the name of the firm did change.) For several years after the successful Xenia hearing the Tucker family sent him Christmas cards, but eventually, he lost contact with Clarence, his father "Popeye," and uncle Neal. Harris also filed a claim with a state agency to recoup financial losses for false imprisonment, but the half-hearted claim was denied. "Clarence wasn't that interested in pursuing it," Harris observed.

Harris continued a successful career in business litigation, representing several major firms. After Tucker v. Ohio, his only other criminal case was in the U.S. 6th Circuit Court, an appeal of Alfred Dean Slack v. United States of America, involving espionage and theft of atomic bomb secrets. Harris retired from litigation in the late 1990s, but continues to be active in business with his own firm, Harris Interests.

::

Adolph Mezger and Millard Schath, the two tough detectives, of whom Harris said "they could have been killers themselves," already were well-known in Cincinnati law enforcement circles when they arrived in Xenia the morning of January 29, 1946, to interrogate Tucker. Mezger, the suave senior partner, retired shortly after the Tucker and Evans case. He died three years later, in 1949.

Schath, on the other hand, continued to have a long, dramatic career in Queen City law enforcement, earning a reputation as a "fast-on-the-trigger" detective. Although he proclaimed, "I'm just tired of it all" when he retired from the Cincinnati police force in 1951, within a few years he was earning more newspaper clippings as a stand-in for an injured officer in suburban Golf Manor. In early 1955, he helped apprehend a bank robber in that community, in the process regaling local reporters with tales of his daring exploits in crime fighting over the years. That "temporary" position lasted until 1957; he died, at age 65, in 1965.

: :

Around 1988 a hefty, balding gentleman in a used-up blue Honda pulled a camping trailer onto a lot in an isolated, wooded trailer park near Hamersville in rural Brown County, east of Cincinnati. There, the friendly old man established a home base, welcoming cats into his trailer (but not dogs), giving candy and little gifts to neighborhood children and building cabinets in area homes. A few years later, when Bill Preston and his wife Barbara set up their mobile home nearby, they took an interest in their elderly neighbor, who introduced himself as Earl Tucker. Over the next several years, the Prestons and Tucker became close friends.

"We hit it off real good. Earl was a likable guy," recalled neighbor Bill Preston. "He usually got along good with everybody."

Preston described Tucker as a uniquely talented woodworker and self-employed carpenter. To earn a living, the old man had fashioned a portable wood-working shed that he would tow to job sites along with his little camper trailer. Then, Tucker would live on the job for the duration of each project.

"I really did admire the man," Preston said. "This guy could do it all—baseboards, cabinets, finish work. He could do anything with a nice piece of wood. I never seen anybody as gifted as he was. Signs, everything."

Tucker also tinkered with electronics, according to Barb Preston, and fashioned elaborate, fanciful devices. "He built an electronic thing to connect to the spiritual world," she remembered. "It reminded me of a CB radio type thing. He said he could talk with the dead."

"I don't know if he believed he could. Sometimes, he acted really serious. Other times, he joked about it."

She also complained that Tucker delighted in inciting conflict between the Prestons. "He was sorta like an aggravator," she said. "He liked to pick on everybody."

Tucker enjoyed banter with Bill over beers in the yard outside their trailers. Dressed in his favored flannel shirts and work pants, held up by suspenders, he would light up Camel cigarettes and unwind tales that included stories of an extremely unhappy relationship with a woman and at least one son. He hinted that he had fled to Brown County to get away from them, Barb said.

He also told of his childhood, growing up among the redwood trees of Oregon, and he impressed Bill Preston, a Vietnam veteran, with fables of military service with the Canadian Special Forces in World War II. Bill had no reason to doubt the stories, and he didn't have reason to question the old man's pronounced limp, which Preston described as "like a wobble, sort of like if he had a bad back or something."

Neither Bill nor Barb ever heard Earl Tucker mention a life behind bars, an attorney in Cincinnati, or court cases.

That is, until one day when Bill had finished mowing Tucker's lawn, a task he did as a favor because Tucker had heart problems. The two shared a few cold beers, and then Tucker "fired up his little blue car and went up to Hamersville to get some ice cream," Bill recalled. The Prestons grew increasingly concerned when the old man didn't return, until the phone rang late that evening. "I figured it was the hospital, 'cause of his bad heart," Bill said. "When they said 'Brown County Detention Center,' I could not believe it."

The Prestons retrieved Tucker and brought him home, but the following morning their friend was furious—"ranting and raving," Bill said. And facing a felony charge.

Tucker told them he had been pulled over by sheriff's deputies, who sought and received permission to search his car. Asked if he was carrying anything in his pockets, the former prison inmate produced a .22 caliber pistol that he carried "because he'd had tools stolen," Preston said. According to Tucker, he voluntarily surrendered it by holding the butt of the gun with his thumb and forefinger and offering it to a deputy. He told Preston the law officers must have felt threatened, because they drew their own weapons.

Tucker's version of the arrest is clearly at odds with the official police report, and was no doubt influenced by the memory of the eerily similar event in Xenia a half-century before.

According to court records, deputies halted Tucker in his Honda when they saw him make a U-turn that evening in front of a grocery in Hamersville. The lawmen testified that they detected the odor of alcohol on the man's breath, but they couldn't do field sobriety tests because of the old man's infirmities. He was instead placed under arrest for driving under the influence, and when he was searched, police found the gun. Tucker was charged with carrying a concealed weapon, a felony.

Tucker was indicted three days later, on July 7, 1997, and arraigned on July 10 in Georgetown, Ohio, where Brown County's old wooden courthouse dominates the town square, surrounded by aged two-story storefronts and lawyers' offices. A young local attorney was appointed to defend the old carpenter, and it's certain that Tucker, recalling his experience with court-appointed attorneys, made life difficult for the defense. According to Bill Preston, his friend swore—literally—that he would not be railroaded (but Tucker neglected to add it would be for a second time). "He was gonna show these sons-of-bitches they weren't going to pull this Brown County bullcrap on him," Preston said. "He fought tooth and nail on his own. He went and did research and wrote letters. He wasn't going to let that public defender get away with nothin'. He said 'you work for me, and this is how it's gonna be!'"

Tucker's insistence apparently had quite an effect, because over the next several months the defendant and his attorney mounted an aggressive defense with detailed research, including a motion to dismiss the case and then a motion to suppress the gun as evidence. The search and subsequent discovery of the firearm occurred without a warrant during an unlawful detention, suggested the document filed by the defense on January 14, 1998. Two weeks later, Judge Alan Corbin agreed, noting in his opinion and judgment that Tucker's U-turn was sufficient to prompt the deputies to investigate, but by itself wasn't sufficient to indicate impaired driving. Thus, without support for the DUI arrest, the gun found in the subsequent search became irrelevant. The case was "a classic dilemma of whether the Court should find for the prosecution because the officers truly did nothing wrong, and perhaps did all that could reasonably be done under the circumstances...; however, it is not this Court's intention to make bad law out of hard cases. This Court will not stretch the law to fit the facts of this case."

Tucker was freed from this grasp of the law, but he could not escape the self-inflicted penalties of his unrefined lifestyle. His health began to fail, and he weakened to the extent that the Prestons took him into their home, where in the next months they watched him dissipate from well over 230 pounds to a wisp of less than 100. In December, Barb insisted that he see a doctor; he was immediately hospitalized for treatment of advanced lung cancer, then moved to a nursing home on the other side of the county. He died there early the morning of February 27, 1999.

The Prestons had Tucker's body cremated. They received, through his will, the trailer he had built to carry his equipment, although it disintegrated when they tried to move it. Bill Preston to this day thinks about his former neighbor. "He was a good old man. I miss him a lot," Preston says.

: :

My father, the Judge who in 1946 imprisoned Clarence Earl Tucker and Ernest Finley Evans, died of a heart attack in the Fall of 1955. Mother died in the Fall of 1962, and with her passing my family's home was left unoccupied. The following January, the temperature dipped to minus 13 degrees, and, because my wife and I had not yet disposed of the old house, when a warm spell arrived, I went to Xenia to check on it.

As I opened the heavy, ornate door of the place, cold air rushed into warm, moisture-laden air inside, and I was immediately enveloped by a ghostly cloud bank. Water dripped from overhead light fixtures. Layers of wallpaper, steamed off of walls and ceilings, draped across the gold damask love seat, antique tables and chairs, and mother's piano. Oak floors were buckled and warped, and doors balked at being opened. What once had been the stately home of a white-haired judge and a graceful lady now lay in ruin.

I stumbled my dazed way through the fog and felt the wrath of God had descended upon my father, my mother, my family, and my home. All was gone. The house was quiet except the dripping: the constant dripping. I envisioned mother playing her piano. I thought I saw my father sitting at his desk, talking on the phone, perhaps to his bookie, perhaps to Prosecutor Marcus Shoup.

I had to leave. I blindly climbed the stairs to find the source of the destruction—a burst water pipe in an unheated part of the third floor—turned off the water, disconnected the electricity, and put the house and its ruined contents up for auction.

I can still see the fog, feel the wet, hear the dripping, and through the mist, I see the ghosts: mother at the piano and the Judge at his desk. Ghosts. Only ghosts.

Postscript

::

Writing this book has opened a floodgate of great memories from childhood to the present, including my relationship with my co-author, Dr. Jeff John. As we grow up we have role models, some of whom we pattern our lives after, and some of whom we divorce ourselves from: "I sure don't want to be like him." My father and the local veterinarian, Dr. Richard Engard, were my two positive models. I wanted to be like my dad, and I wanted to be a vet. For Tucker and Evans, I believe the role models were the gangsters of the early thirties.

Education, marriage, raising four children, and financial security took precedence over thinking much about Tucker and Evans until 1995, when we moved to Cedarville, Ohio. I became curious about the results of this case far in my past, and started going to the Xenia library to investigate the fate of the two young men. One thing led to another. I met Jeff and, at his suggestion, we started writing this book.

The world would be no better nor worse if the two had been executed for their crime, but Tucker did not deserve the twenty-one years he spent in prison. After his release, he was persecuted repeatedly for his role in the murder and led an unhappy life until he died in 1999. I believe Evans became a born-again Christian after his near-death experience while incarcerated. He became a model prisoner, was released from prison, and had but a brief time to live normally before he died in 1975. God rest their souls.

FLJ
June 2010

Annotated Bibliography

::

"A Historical Look at Hiram College," Archives and Special Collections, Hiram College Library. http://library.hiram.edu/Archives/history.htm

Discusses the college and the Intensive Study Plan under which Army Air Corps personnel attended Hiram College during World War II.

"All 4 Local Contests on GOP Ballot at Primary," *The Evening Gazette*, May 1, 1948, p. 1.

Pre-primary story noting extraordinary numbers of registrations and "spirited campaigning" for county prosecutor position.

American Bar Association Project on Minimum Standards for Criminal Justice. *Standards Related to Post-Conviction Remedies.* New York: American Bar Association, 1967.

Discussion of the background of post-conviction remedies as a needed alternative to habeas corpus actions.

"Anderson, Joseph Dies; Was Murder Witness." *Yellow Springs (Ohio) News*, Jan. 18, 1967.

Obituary indicating the death of Anderson, the state's last surviving witness in the murder trial, "may have a bearing on the appeal for parole of C. Tucker."

Anderson, Maureen A. "The First Visalia," *Los Tulares*, Quarterly Bulletin of the Tulare County Historical Society. Sept. 1996.
Description of the Kentucky community where Ernest F. Evans grew up.

"Aultman and Bahns Provide GOP Upsets," *The Evening Gazette*, May 5, 1948, pp. 1–2.
Voting results in GOP primary election of 1948.

Aultman, J. Decision, State of Ohio, plaintiff v. Clarence Tucker, defendant. Case No. 8101. Oct. 13, 1967.
Greene County Court reviews findings from February 14, 1967 hearing and sets aside the original sentence imposed upon Clarence Tucker, and grants a new trial.

"Auto Theft Thug Shoots Deputy Sheriff Earl Confer," *The Cedarville Herald*, Feb. 1, 1946.
Front-page account of the crime from the point of view of the weekly newspaper in the village where Evans and Tucker had stopped for breakfast before the event.

Baxter, Joan. Interview. Xenia, Ohio, July 17, 2008.
Joan Baxter is the former director of Greene County Historical Society.

Boertlein, John. *Ohio Confidential.* Cincinnati: Clerisy Press, 2008.
Outlines famous Ohio criminal cases, including the Sam Sheppard murder case and controversies surrounding Gov. James Rhodes.

Boryczka. Raymond and Cary, Lorin Lee. *No Strength Without Union.* Columbus: Ohio Historical Society, 1982.
Includes impact of postwar strikes in '45–'46 statistics; charts: "Work Stoppages in U.S. and Ohio" (p. 285), and "Man-hours lost in work stoppages" (p. 294).

Boys' Industrial School Inmate Case Record GR3979, Case Serial No. 41021 (1943). Ohio Historical Society Archives, Columbus, Ohio.
Lists names, date of entry, committing authority and various demographic and personal data about inmates of the Ohio boys' reformatory.

"Brigadier General Charles E. Yeager," Check-Six.com. http://www.check-six.com/lib/bios/Charles E_Yeager Biography.htm.
Official Air Force biography of test pilot "Chuck" Yeager, who served as an instructor pilot at the base where Evans was stationed during World War II.

Brock, Lynn. Interview, September 2, 2008.

Brock is custodian of the Strobridge Collection, held at Cedarville University. The collection provides details about the history of Cedarville, Ohio.

Burns, Bob. "'Real Happy' At News," *Xenia Daily Gazette*, Oct. 14, 1967, p. 1.

Gazette reporter breaks news of appeal's success to Tucker in prison.

Certificate of Death, Clarence Earl Tucker. Ohio Department of Health, Vital Statistics.

Provides cause of death, address, and vital statistics of Tucker at his death in 1999.

Certificate of Death, Ernest F. Evans. Ohio Department of Health, Division of Vital Statistics.

Provides cause of death, address, and vital statistics of Evans at his death in 1975.

Cincinnati Bar Association, Geo. Stimson, ed. *The Law in Southwest Ohio.* Cincinnati Bar Association, 1972. p. 378.

Alton F. Brown employs "unusual and devastating tactics" in winning the 1908 political race for Warren County prosecutor.

"City's Bread Box Runs Low as Meat Picture Brightens," *The Cincinnati Enquirer*, Jan. 21, 1946, p. 1.
Bakery workers threaten a bread "famine" in the Cincinnati area.

"Closed Theater Is Reopened Friday." *The Evening Gazette*, Feb. 5, 1943, p. 1.
Contemporary news report in aftermath of January 30 race riot in Xenia.

"Convicted Killers Removed to Prison; Carved Gun Found," *The Evening Gazette*, April 25, 1946, pp. 1-2.
Police claim to have found a replica of a revolver in Clarence Tucker's Xenia jail cell; description and quotes from conclusion of trial and sentencing.

"Courtroom Scene At Murder Trial," *The Evening Gazette*, April 24, 1946, p. 1.
Photograph and accompanying lengthy caption describing Evans, Tucker, and defense team at the murder trial.

"Crime Records of 2 Suspects Are Disclosed." *The Evening Gazette*, January 30, 1946, p. 1.
Includes quotes from parents of Evans and Tucker concerning their backgrounds.

Cummings, Walter. Interview, Cedarville, Ohio. March 3, 2009.

Mr. Cummings is a 103-year-old citizen of Cedarville who recalls the restaurant visited by Tucker and Evans in 1946.

"Deputy Earl Confer, Killed in Xenia Gun Battle, Former Resident Here." *Yellow Springs News*, Jan. 31, 1946.

Report and obituary in the weekly newspaper of Yellow Springs, the community near Xenia that was the hometown of Deputy Confer.

"Deputy Killed, 2 Shot in Xenia Pistol Battle." *Cincinnati Post*, Jan. 29, 1946.

Overview of the Xenia shooting, with emphasis on Cincinnati connections of the two arrested youths.

"Deputy Sheriff's Slayers Charged With Shooting in Madison County," (London, Ohio) *Madison Press*, Jan. 29, 1946, pp. 1–2.

London, Ohio, sheriff describes damage by mysterious shooters in the community the night before the Xenia shootings.

"Detective Millard Schath to Retire After 27 Years in Police Department," *Cincinnati Post*, Aug. 7, 1951, p. 3. "Criminals' Nemesis Retiring; 'Tired of It,' Detective Says," *The Cincinnati Enquirer*, Aug. 8, 1951, p. 13.

Reports in both papers announce retirement and recount some adventures on the Cincinnati police force of a well-known detective, one of two who interrogated Tucker.

DiSalle, Michael V. with L.G. Blochman. *The Power of Life or Death*. New York: Random House, 1965.

DiSalle, Ohio governor 1959–1963, opposed the death penalty and recorded his opinions about it in this book, which includes a chapter and further comments describing the use of prison labor at the Ohio governor's mansion.

Elebash, C.C. "Was it the Air Corps or Army Air Force in WWII?" Army Air Forces Historical Association. www.aafha.org

Discussion of accurate World War II air service branches and unit designations.

"Evans and Tucker Guilty; Both Given Life Sentences." *The Evening Gazette*, April 24, 1946, pp. 1–2.

Coverage of the trial's second day with descriptions of verdict, sentencing.

Fact of Death form, Birth and Death Record, Oregon Department of Health Services

Lists approximate date of death and location, in Portland, Oregon, of Tucker's mother.

Final Payment Work Sheet, Evans, Ernest F. U.S. War Department, 1945.

Includes name, address, serial numbers, dates, and locations of enlistment and discharge, muster-out pay.

"Funeral Service for Judge Rankin Saturday." *Washington Court House Record-Herald*, May 1, 1953, p. 1.

Relates Judge Rankin's obituary, including legal precedents set and legal decisions.

Ford, Jim. Interview. November 15, 2007.

First black member of Greene County Commission and friend of Deputy Joseph Anderson, wounded in the Xenia shootout.

"Geo. Smith Backed For Appointment to Election Board," *The Evening Gazette*, Jan. 25, 1946, p. 1.

Background of one of the attorneys appointed to defend Tucker and Evans.

"Grand Jurors Open Probe Into Slaying," *The Evening Gazette*, Feb. 7, 1946, p. 1.

Report on Greene County grand jury session, highlighted by consideration of the Tucker and Evans case.

Haas, Christopher, M.D. Interview, October 10, 2008.
Dr. Haas treated Tucker in 1999 and signed the death certificate.

Hake, Dorothy. "News About Food," *The Cincinnati Enquirer*, Jan. 26, 1946, p. 6.
This column discusses the availability of food items in Cincinnati markets, local food prices, and shopping tips for bargains in groceries.

Harris, Irving. Interviews, Cincinnati, Ohio, September 6, 2006; April 18, 2007; December 5, 2007; October 20, 2008.
Harris represented Clarence Tucker during the 1950s and early 1960s in his repeated requests for a new trial, and in the hearing in Greene County, December 1966 to February 1967, which resulted in Tucker's release.

Hidy, Logan A. "A Study of Automobile Theft and of the Juvenile Involved, with a case study of 136 boys committed to the Boys' Industrial School, Lancaster, Ohio, Following the offense of Automobile Theft." M.A. Thesis, Ohio University, 1951.
Describes typical profiles and motivation of youths convicted of auto theft and sentenced to the Ohio juvenile detention facility.

Hill, June Marie Edwards. Interview, Garrettsville, Ohio, September 6, 2008.
June Edwards was the girlfriend Evans visited in Akron, Ohio, prior to the Xenia incident.

Hoover, J.C., Barnes, J.D., Jones, W.D., Conover, C.R., Wright, J.W., Leiter, C.A., Bradford, J.E., Culkins, W.C., eds. *Memoirs of the Miami Valley, V. III.* Chicago, Robert O. Law Co., 1919. p. 111.
Alton F. Brown joins law firm of Hamilton and Brown. Brown later becomes Probate Judge.

Hummel, L. Interview. December 17, 2008.
Hummel, a Records Analyst, Indiana Commission on Public Records, unearthed a record card for Ernest Evans' incarceration at the Indiana Boys' School at Plainfield.

Inmate Case Records, Boys' Industrial School, 1943-1944, Vol. 59, p. 11. Ohio Historical Society Archives/ Library.
Case record of Clarence Tucker's time at the Ohio Boy's Industrial School. Lancaster, Ohio.

Inmate Manual: Handbook of Information and Regulations Governing Men Committed to the Ohio State Penitentiary. Rev. Ed. Columbus, Ohio: Ohio Department of Hygiene and Correction, 1961.
Booklet giving rules and advice for inmates, provided when they were booked into the Ohio Penitentiary.

James, Howard. *Children in Trouble: A National Scandal.* New York: D McKay Co., 1970.
Description of extreme treatment of boys in the Indiana Boys' School at Plainfield, Indiana.

Johnson, Judge Frank L. Correspondence with Irving Harris, June 30, 1953.
Letter to Clarence Tucker's attorney, in which Judge Johnson defends the original trial and reveals that two of the judges of the tribunal sought the death penalty.

Jordan, Jack. "21 Years is a Long Time—In Pen," *Xenia Daily Gazette*, Feb. 10, 1967, p. 1.
The reporter who covered the original Evans/Tucker trial in 1946, now elevated to editor and general manager of the Xenia daily newspaper, writes about his memories of the case and the changes he sees in Tucker twenty-one years later.

"Judge Alton F. Brown Assists in Xenia Trial." *Warren County News*, April 25, 1946, p. 1.
Announces that Judge Brown will serve on three-judge tribunal in Greene County.

"Judge Alton F. Brown Dies After Lingering Illness." (Lebanon, Ohio) *Western Star*, March 6, 1951, p. 1.
Obituary, describing Judge Brown as "a leading figure in legal circles in Lebanon."

"Judge Johnson Dies; Served As County Jurist 16 Years," *Xenia Daily Gazette*, Sept. 29, 1955.
Lengthy obituary of Judge Frank L. Johnson, who presided in the trial of Tucker and Evans.

"Judge Rankin is Sitting in Murder Trial." *Washington Court House Record-Herald*, April 24, 1946, p. 5.
Announces Judge Harry M. Rankin of Fayette County will serve on three-judge tribunal in Greene County.

"Jury Indicts 2 Cincinnati Youths in Deputy Slaying," *The Evening Gazette*, Feb. 9, 1946, p. 1.
Tucker and Evans indicted for first-degree murder; jury commission instructed to draw sixty names for a jury, and attorney Sam Kelly of Dayton named to assist Prosecutor Marcus Shoup.

"Killers Given Life Sentence." *Washington Court House Record-Herald*, April 25, 1946, p. 14.
Summary of trial, with quote by Counsel G. W. Smith.

"Life Sentences Given To Two Cincinnatians In Slaying of Officer," *The Cincinnati Enquirer*, April 24, 1946, p. 1.
Associate Press report summarizing the trial.

Lippman, Walter. "The State of the Union." *The Cincinnati Enquirer*, Jan. 23, 1946, p. 4.
Famous newspaper columnist summarizes the country's postwar economic and social situation prior to the President's State of the Union message.

Lore, David. "Inside the Pen," *The Columbus Dispatch*, Oct. 28, 1984. http://www.drc.state.oh.us/WEB/histop.htm
Overview of life in the Ohio Penitentiary, with a focus on the period after World War II until the prison was closed in 1984.

Mairos, Mary Alice, Ian Adams, Dianne McElwain, and Ted Strickland. *Our First Family's Home: The Ohio Governor's Residence and Heritage Garden*. Athens, Ohio: Ohio University Press, 2008.
Description and history of the Governor's Mansion in Bexley, Ohio.

Mainwaring, Michal. Interview, January 12, 2008.
Mainwaring was the daughter of the registrar of motor vehicles in the administration of James Rhodes and an employee in the statehouse during the Rhodes administrations.

"Man Convicted of Murder In County Seeks Release," *Xenia Daily Gazette*, Dec. 20, 1966, p. 1.
Newspaper report of Attorney Harris's petition for hearing to vacate Tucker's original sentence.

McCatherine, Tom. "Tucker Conviction Set Aside By Judge," *Xenia Daily Gazette*, Oct. 14, 1967, p. 1.
Newspaper report announcing appeal decision, and announcing that the county prosecutor would not pursue a new trial, thus freeing Tucker.

McElroy, John M. Correspondence with Clarence Tucker, June 3, 1966.
The executive assistant to Governor James Rhodes explains to Tucker why a request for commutation was denied by the Parole Board and suggests alternatives for clemency such as the Post-Conviction Remedy Statute that Tucker ultimately used to secure his release.

Metzger, Hal. "Retired Detective Helps in Snagging of Suspect; Schath Career Colorful," *The Cincinnati Enquirer*, Feb. 3, 1955, p. 16.
Profile of the longtime Cincinnati police officer who helped interrogate Tucker after the Xenia shooting.

"Millard C. Schath, 65, Dies; Retired Cincinnati Detective," *Cincinnati Post and Times-Star*, Jan. 20, 1965, p. 4.
Obituary of famous detective who interrogated Tucker.

Moore, Sue. Interview, July 10, 2008.
Moore is the daughter of Governor James Rhodes and lived in the governor's mansion in the mid-1960s, when Ernest Evans worked as a prison trusty at the mansion.

Morrow, Jennifer S., Interview and Correspondence, September 22, 2008.

Morrow is College Archivist, Hiram College Archives and Special Collections.

"Murder Charge Filed In Shooting in Xenia," *The Cincinnati Enquirer,* Feb. 1, 1946.

Associated Press account prior to grand jury indictments.

Ohio Legislative Acts Passed and Joint Resolutions Adopted. (January 4, 1965 to September 1, 1965). vol. 131.

Includes the Act establishing Ohio's post-conviction remedies used by Tucker to win a new hearing.

Ohio Federal Writers' Project. *Cincinnati: A Guide to the Queen City and Its Neighbors.* Cincinnati: The Wiesen-Hart Press, 1943.

A comprehensive World War II-era guide to the city.

Ohio Governor Pardon Record, 1963–1975, Pardons, Reprieves and Commutations. Ohio Historical Society, Archives/Library.

Parole Board application for commutation for Ernest Evans, with comments by parole board.

Ohio Penitentiary Register of Prisoners, p. 370. Ohio Historical Society Archives/Library.
Handwritten entries signing Evans and Tucker into the Ohio Penitentiary, with their crime and sentence, and the prisoner number assigned to each.

"1-15 Year Term is Meted Out in Burglary Case." *Warren County News*, Feb. 1, 1945, p. 1.
Example of Judge Alton F. Brown's sentencing, in this case, up to fifteen years imprisonment for burglary.

"Oznl H. Cornwell, 79; Xenia police ex-chief." *Xenia Daily Gazette*, Aug. 16, 1972.
Lengthy obituary.

Page, William H., ed. *Page's Ohio General Code, Annotated.* Lifetime Edition. Vol. 10. Cincinnati: The W.H. Anderson Company, 1938.
The Ohio Criminal Code in effect in 1946, with commentary, citations to supporting court cases.

"Parents 'Never Lost Faith' In 21-Year Battle," *Xenia Daily Gazette*, Oct. 14, 1967, p. 1.
Comments by Tucker's father and attorney upon the announcement of his pending release from prison.

Plainfield Juvenile Correction Facility, Wikipedia, http://en.wikipedia.org/wiki/PlainfieldCorrectional Facility.

General description of the facility that housed Ernest Evans prior to his enlistment.

Preston, Barbara. Interview, Hamersville, Ohio, May 20, 2009.

Barbara Preston cared for Clarence Earl Tucker in her home until his hospitalization before his death.

Preston, Bill. Interview, Mt. Orab, Ohio, May 18, 2009.

Preston was a neighbor of Tucker in his later years.

"Private Detectives Demanded to Sift Night Spot Gambling," *The Cincinnati Enquirer*, Jan. 29, 1946, p. 2.

A Newport, Kentucky attorney accuses the Newport city officials of corruption.

Ralls v. State. 40 O. App. 69, 177 N.E. 787.

Precedent-setting court case in which a defendant's written confession and testimony that he entered into a conspiracy with a confederate to fight with police officers was held to justify a conviction of first-degree murder.

Record of arrests, Xenia Police Department, Jan. 29, 1946. Local Government Records, Wright State University Special Collections and Archives.

Police booking record for arrests the morning of the Xenia shooting incident.

Record of births, Wallowa County, Oregon, 1925, p. 50A-B.
Handwritten record including name and birth date of Clarence Earl Tucker, father's and mother's ages, birthplaces, and occupations.

"Sheriff's Deputy Killed in Gunfight on Xenia Street," *The Evening Gazette*, Jan. 29, 1946, p. 1.
Initial report in the local Xenia daily newspaper describing in detail the crime, victims, and perpetrators.

"Sheriff's Deputy Shot To Death In Xenia Gun Fight," *Dayton Daily News*, Jan. 30, 1946, p. 1.
An account in the Dayton newspaper of the Xenia felony crime.

"'Shooting Pact' Charged at Trial," *The Evening Gazette*, April 23, 1946, p. 1.
News report of trial's first-day activities.

"Shooting Pact Testimony Upheld At Xenia," *The Herald*, April 24, 1946, p. 1.
Dayton newspaper report of the 1946 trial, with photos of Evans in a wheelchair and Tucker being released from handcuffs.

"Slayers Are Taken To Pen," *The Evening Gazette*, Apr. 20, 1946, p. 2.
Sheriff Walton Spahr transports the pair convicted of murder to the Ohio Penitentiary, retracing some of the path they took into Xenia.

State of Ohio, plaintiff v. Clarence Tucker, et al., defendants. Court of Common Pleas, County of Greene, State of Ohio, Case No. 8101. Brief on Behalf of Petitioner to Vacate or Set Aside Sentence Under Section 2953.21, Ohio Revised Code. Dec. 20, 1966. *Presentation of legal arguments supporting a new trial for Clarence E. Tucker.*

State of Ohio, plaintiff v. Clarence Tucker, defendant. In the Court of Common Pleas, Greene County, Ohio, Oct. 13, 1967. Case No. 8101. Decision. *Ruling by Judge Dan M. Aultman to set aside the original verdict convicting Tucker, with explanation of the reasons for the ruling.*

State of Ohio, plaintiff v. Clarence Tucker, defendant. In the Court of Common Pleas, Greene County, Ohio, December 20, 1966. Motion to vacate or set aside sentence, in Assorted Court Records, Greene County Records Center and Archives, Xenia, Ohio. *Legal papers including petition for new trial and approval of application for habeas corpus, to bring Tucker for court hearing.*

State of Ohio, plaintiff v. Clarence Tucker, defendant. In the Court of Common Pleas, Greene County, Ohio, Feb. 14, 1967. *Testimony in the hearing for a new trial for Clarence Tucker.*

State of Ohio, plaintiff v. Earl C. Tucker, defendant. In the Court of Common Pleas, Brown County, Ohio, Jan. 31, 1998.
Opinion and judgment entry for Case No. 972077, involving Clarence Earl Tucker charged with carrying a concealed weapon.

State of Ohio, Plaintiff, v. Ernest F. Evans and Clarence E. Tucker, Defendants, No. 8101. Court of Common Pleas, Greene County, in Assorted Court Records, Greene County Records Center and Archives, Xenia, Ohio.
Assorted legal documents including indictment, pleas, appointment of defense attorneys, formal request of waiver of trial by jury, application for joint trial of defendants, verdict, sentence of life imprisonment, and warrant to convey prisoners to Ohio penitentiary.

"Strikes at a glance," *Cincinnati Enquirer*, Jan. 21,1946, p. 1.
Thumbnail sketches of strikes across U.S. in bakeries, meatpacking plants, Westinghouse, General Electric, and General Motors factories, and transportation.

"Strikes Start at Midnight In Cincinnati Steel Plants" *The Cincinnati Enquirer*, Jan. 21, 1946, p. 1.
11,600 steelworkers threaten strike in Greater Cincinnati area plants.

"There's Too Much Now: Gasoline Price Cuts Begin to Trickle in As Surplus Stocks Soar," *The Cincinnati Enquirer*, Jan. 23, 1946, p. 13.
Standard Oil Company cuts prices as American Petroleum Institute estimates record amounts of fuel in storage.

"Three-Judge Court Okayed," *The Evening Gazette*, March 29, 1946, p. 1.
Ohio Chief Justice Carl Weygandt announces he allows judge tribunal in the case, and tells Judge Johnson he will appoint two other jurists.

"Tip-Off On Ohio Suspects Given to Cincinnati Oil Station Man." *The Cincinnati Enquirer*, Jan. 30, 1946, p. 1.
Relates the coincidental mission of Detectives Mezger and Schath, en route to Dayton when they were called to interview Tucker immediately after the Xenia shooting incident.

"Tucker Set Free In Court Today," *Xenia Daily Gazette*, Oct. 20, 1967, p. 1.
Final court papers signed, releasing Tucker, who comments that he wants to "drop out of sight."

Transcript of Testimony, State of Ohio v. Ernest F. Evans and Clarence E. Tucker, Court of Common Pleas, Greene County, Ohio.
Complete official record of testimony in the 1946 trial.

"Two Cincinnati Men Are Held in Officer's Slaying At Xenia," *The Cincinnati Enquirer*, Jan. 30, 1946, p. 1.
Cincinnati news account of the crime and arrests.

U.S. Department of Commerce. *Bureau of the Census.* Census of Population and Housing, 1940 Census. Vol. 4, Part 4; and Census of Population and Housing, 1950 Census, Vol. 2, Ohio, Part 35.
Provides statistics on white and minority population of Xenia, Ohio, per decennial census.

U.S. Department of Commerce. Bureau of the Census. Historical Statistics of the United States, Pt. 1, 1975.
Statistics describing price increases '45–'46 listed under Retail Prices of Selected Foods in U.S. Cities (p. 213).

U.S. Department of Commerce. Bureau of the Census. 1920 Census records, Oregon. http://www.census.gov/prod/www/abs/decennial/1920.htm
Information on the background of Claude Tucker, grandfather of Clarence Earl Tucker.

Vondruska, Tom. "Breaking color barriers in area restaurants was battle." *Xenia Daily Gazette*, Jan. 15, 1986, p. 3A.
Recollections of efforts to desegregate popular dining establishments in Xenia.

———. "Desegregating Xenia theaters: Effort began in early 1940s and continued into the 1960s." *Xenia Daily Gazette*, Jan. 15, 1986.
Examination of Jim Crow attitudes in Xenia and tactics used in events that led to desegregation.

Wilkes, Donald E. Jr. *Federal and State Postconviction Remedies and Relief.* Norcross, Georgia: The Harrison Company Publishers, 1983.
Explanation of post-conviction remedies in courts generally, and discussion of laws enacted in each state.

"Witness In Slaying Case Dies," *Dayton Daily News*, Jan. 13, 1967.
Reports the death of Joseph Anderson, the deputy wounded in the shooting who later agreed to testify on behalf of Tucker. Anderson died about a week before the hearing with Judge Aultman.

Wooden, James. *Weeping in the Playtime of Others*, 2nd. ed. Columbus, Ohio: The Ohio State University Press, 2000.
Includes discussion of conditions at Indiana School for Boys in the context of Charles Manson's incarceration there, some fifteen years after Ernest Evans.

Xenia and Vicinity Telephone Directory. The Ohio Bell Telephone Co., June 1944. Greene County Historical Society, Xenia, Ohio.
Phone numbers, addresses in Greene County as of 1944.

"Xenia Attorney Marcus W. Shoup succumbs at 69," *Xenia Daily Gazette*, Nov. 22, 1971.
Obituary of former three-term Greene County Prosecuting Attorney who prosecuted Tucker and Evans.

"Xenia Theater Closed Under Legal Orders," *The Evening Gazette*, Feb. 1, 1943.
Contemporary news coverage of civil disturbance in Xenia caused by segregated theaters.

Zimmerman, Richard G. *Plain Dealing: Ohio Politics and Journalism.* Kent, Ohio: Kent State University Press, 2001.
In-depth discussion of Ohio politics, including descriptions of activities within the administrations of Governor James Rhodes at the time Ernest Evans was released from prison.

———. "Rhodes's First Eight Years, 1963–1971." In *Ohio Politics*, edited by Alexander P. Lamis, 59–83. Kent, Ohio: The Kent State University Press, 1994.
A comprehensive overview of Rhodes and the character of his first administration.

Author Biographies

::

Jeffrey Alan John Ph.D. (pictured in back), teaches journalism as an associate professor in the Department of Communication at Wright State University in Dayton, Ohio. He experienced Xenia, Ohio, as a newspaper reporter there, and then was a magazine editor and public relations writer. A Dayton native, he currently lives in Bellbrook, Ohio, with his wife, Karin Avila-John, and teenaged triplet sons.

Frank L. Johnson D.V.M. (pictured in front), the son of Greene County, Ohio's Common Pleas Court judge, graduated from The Ohio State University College of Veterinary Medicine in 1952 and practiced veterinary medicine in the Cincinnati area. He lives in Kettering, Ohio, with his wife, Pat.

brandon haskins | design

Brandon Haskins (1988-2010)
Chief Creative Officer
Clay Bridges Publishing

Brandon Haskins, the skilled designer behind the cover of this book, tragically passed away on July 8, 2010. This book displays his final cover design. We are pleased to offer this publication to the world as a living memorial to him and his work. May we all live as creatively and passionately as he did.

"A life lived in fear...
is a life half-lived."

GRAPHIC DESIGN | INTERIOR DESIGN | INTERIOR DECOR

www.ingramcontent.com/pod-product-compliance
Lightning Source LLC
LaVergne TN
LVHW091049080826
845145LV00002B/680

* 9 7 8 1 6 3 2 9 6 2 2 2 5 *